Women Kings

Abednego Abbey

Published by Abednego Abbey, 2023.

WOMEN KINGS

First edition. December 4, 2023.

Copyright © 2023 Abednego Abbey.

ISBN: 979-8223395423

Written by Abednego Abbey.

Table of Contents

Preface 1

Introduction 3

Queen Amina of Zazzau 7

Queen Nzinga of Ndongo and Matamba............................ 15

Queen Yaa Asentewaa of Ashanti Empire........................... 26

Queen Makeda of Sheba 37

Queen Ranavalona I of Madagascar 45

Queen Amanirenas of Kush 54

Queen Nandi of the Zulu Kingdom.................................... 61

Queen Kahina of the Berber Kingdom................................ 69

Conclusion.. 78

Preface

"**W**omen Kings" is a captivating exploration of the remarkable female warriors who shaped the history of Africa. This book delves into the lives and legacies of ten extraordinary queens who defied societal norms and led their kingdoms with courage and strength. From Queen Amina of Zazzau to Queen Kahina of the Berber Kingdom, each chapter unveils the fascinating stories of these powerful women and their indelible impact on African history. Through meticulous research and engaging storytelling, "Women Kings" sheds light on the often overlooked contributions of these remarkable leaders and celebrates their enduring legacy.

In the first chapter, "Introduction to Women Kings," readers are introduced to the concept of warrior queens and the historical context in which they emerged. The importance of female warriors is explored, highlighting their unique roles in African societies and the significance of their contributions. Additionally, an overview of African warrior queens sets the stage for the subsequent chapters, providing a glimpse into the diverse range of queens to be explored.

Subsequent chapters delve into the lives of specific warrior queens, beginning with Queen Amina of Zazzau. Readers are taken on a journey through her early life, her ascension to power, and her military campaigns and conquests. The chapter also examines her lasting legacy and the impact she had on her kingdom and beyond. Similar in structure, subsequent chapters explore the lives of other influential warrior queens such as Queen Nzinga of Ndongo and Matamba, Queen Yaa Asantewaa of the Ashanti Empire, and Queen Makeda of Sheba.

As the book progresses, readers are introduced to the stories of Queen Ranavalona I of Madagascar, Queen Amanirenas of Kush, Queen Nandi of the Zulu Kingdom, and Queen Kahina of the Berber Kingdom. Each chapter delves into their rise to power, their military strategies, and the lasting impact they had on their respective societies. The book concludes with a thought-provoking chapter that reflects on the overall impact of warrior queens in African history, the lessons we can learn from their lives, and the importance of continuing the legacy of female empowerment.

Introduction

Defining the women kings.

Warrior Queens, also known as female warriors, are women who have displayed exceptional courage, leadership, and military prowess in the context of warfare. These remarkable women have defied societal norms and expectations, challenging the traditional roles assigned to women in their respective cultures. Warrior Queens have emerged throughout history, leaving an indelible mark on the world with their bravery, strategic thinking, and ability to command armies.

In the African context, Warrior Queens have played a significant role in shaping the continent's history. These formidable women have led armies, defended their kingdoms, and fought against colonization and oppression. They have become symbols of strength, resilience, and female empowerment, inspiring generations to come.

The term "Warrior Queen" encompasses a diverse range of women who have exhibited exceptional military skills and leadership qualities. These women hail from various African regions and cultures, each with their unique stories and contributions. From the powerful Queen Amina of Zazzau to the legendary Queen Makeda of Sheba, these Warrior Queens have left an indelible mark on African history.

While the term "Warrior Queen" primarily refers to women who have engaged in military activities, it is important to note that their influence extends beyond the battlefield. These women were not only skilled warriors but also effective rulers, diplomats, and strategists. They demonstrated their ability to govern and protect their kingdoms, often in the face of formidable challenges.

The concept of Warrior Queens challenges the traditional gender roles and stereotypes prevalent in many societies. These women defied societal expectations that confined women to domestic roles and proved that they were equally capable of leading armies and making strategic decisions. By breaking these barriers, Warrior Queens paved the way for future generations of women to assert their rights and claim their place in society.

The stories of Warrior Queens highlight the importance of recognizing and celebrating the contributions of women in history. By acknowledging their achievements, we challenge the notion that history is solely shaped by men. Warrior Queens serve as role models for women and girls, inspiring them to pursue their dreams, overcome obstacles, and make a difference in their communities.

By studying the lives of these Warrior Queens, we gain a deeper understanding of the historical context in which they lived and the challenges they faced. Their stories provide valuable insights into the complexities of African history, shedding light on the struggles, triumphs, and resilience of the continent's diverse cultures.

In following chapters, we will embark on a journey through time, exploring the lives of Warrior Queens who left an indelible mark on African history. Their stories will inspire and empower, reminding us of the strength and courage that lies within every individual, regardless of gender. Let us now delve into the fascinating world of African Warrior Queens and uncover the remarkable stories that have shaped the course of history.

Historical Context

THROUGHOUT HISTORY, the role of women in warfare has often been overlooked or underestimated. However, in ancient Africa, there were numerous instances of powerful and influential female warriors who played significant roles in shaping the continent's history. These warrior queens defied societal norms and led their people in times of conflict, displaying exceptional bravery, strategic thinking, and military prowess.

To understand the historical context of these warrior queens, it is essential to delve into the ancient civilizations of Africa. The continent was home to a diverse range of cultures, each with its own unique traditions, social structures, and political systems. From the mighty empires of Kush and Ashanti to the ancient kingdoms of Zazzau and Ndongo, Africa's history is rich with tales of powerful female leaders who defied gender norms and fought alongside their male counterparts.

In many African societies, women held positions of power and authority, and their contributions to warfare were highly valued. These warrior queens emerged in a time when Africa was facing external threats, such as colonization and invasion, as well as internal conflicts and power struggles. Their leadership and military skills were crucial in defending their people, preserving their cultures, and ensuring the survival of their kingdoms.

The historical context of these warrior queens is also intertwined with the broader historical events that shaped Africa. From the ancient civilizations of Egypt and Nubia to the Arab conquests and European colonization, Africa experienced a series of political, social, and cultural transformations. These changes often led to conflicts and power struggles, creating opportunities for exceptional leaders to rise to prominence.

One significant historical context for the emergence of warrior queens in Africa was the trans-Saharan trade routes. These trade routes connected Africa with the Arab world and facilitated the exchange of goods, ideas, and technologies. As a result, African societies became exposed to different military strategies, weapons, and tactics, which influenced their approach to warfare.

Another important historical context was the arrival of European powers on the African continent. The scramble for Africa in the late 19th and early 20th centuries led to the colonization of vast territories by European nations. This period of colonialism brought about significant changes in African societies, including the erosion of traditional power structures and the imposition of foreign rule. In response to these challenges, women kings emerged as symbols of resistance and defiance against colonial oppression.

Furthermore, the historical context of these warrior queens is closely tied to the social and cultural dynamics of their respective societies. In many African cultures, women held positions of authority and played vital roles in governance, religion, and warfare. These societies recognized the inherent strength and capabilities of women, allowing them to rise to positions of leadership during times of conflict.

The historical context of warrior queens in Africa is a testament to the resilience and strength of African women throughout history. These remarkable individuals defied societal expectations, shattered gender norms, and led their people with courage and determination. Their stories serve as a reminder of the significant contributions women have made to African history and the importance of recognizing and celebrating their achievements.

Queen Amina of Zazzau

Early Life and Ascension to Power

Queen Amina of Zazzau, also known as Queen Aminatu, was a legendary warrior queen who ruled over the ancient kingdom of Zazzau, located in what is now modern-day Nigeria. Her story is one of courage, strength, and determination, as she defied societal norms and rose to power in a male-dominated world.

Birth and Lineage

AMINA WAS BORN IN THE late 16th century, into the royal family of Zazzau. She was the daughter of Queen Bakwa Turunku, a renowned woman king herself, who had established Zazzau as a powerful kingdom. Amina's birthright as the daughter of the queen ensured her a place of prominence within the kingdom and set the stage for her future as a warrior queen.

Early Training and Education

FROM A YOUNG AGE, AMINA was exposed to the art of warfare and leadership. She received extensive training in combat skills, horse riding, archery, and military strategy. Her mother, Queen Bakwa Turunku, recognized her daughter's potential and personally oversaw her training, ensuring that Amina would be well-prepared to take on the responsibilities of ruling Zazzau.

Amina's education was not limited to military training alone. She also received a comprehensive education in politics, diplomacy, and governance. Her mother believed that a well-rounded education would equip Amina to be a capable and effective ruler, capable of leading her people both on and off the battlefield.

Ascension to Power

WHEN QUEEN BAKWA TURUNKU passed away, Amina ascended to the throne of Zazzau. Her ascension was not without challenges, as there were those who doubted her ability to rule due to her gender. However, Amina quickly proved her detractors wrong by displaying her exceptional leadership skills and military prowess.

Amina's first act as queen was to strengthen the kingdom's defenses and expand its territories. She embarked on a series of military campaigns, leading her army to victory after victory. Her strategic brilliance and fearless approach to warfare earned her the respect and admiration of her soldiers and subjects alike.

Military Reforms and Innovations

DURING HER REIGN, AMINA implemented several military reforms that revolutionized the way warfare was conducted in Zazzau. She introduced new weapons and tactics, improving the efficiency and effectiveness of her army. Amina also established a network of well-fortified garrison towns throughout the kingdom, ensuring the security of her territories and facilitating trade and communication.

One of Amina's most significant military innovations was the introduction of cavalry units composed entirely of female warriors. These fierce and skilled horsewomen, known as the "Cavalry Daughters," played a crucial role in Amina's military campaigns. Their speed, agility, and mastery of mounted combat gave the Zazzau army a distinct advantage on the battlefield.

Diplomacy and Alliances

AMINA'S REIGN WAS NOT solely defined by military conquests. She also recognized the importance of diplomacy and formed strategic alliances with neighboring kingdoms. Through her diplomatic efforts, Amina forged strong alliances that helped secure the borders of Zazzau and ensured the prosperity of her kingdom.

Amina's diplomatic skills were particularly evident in her relationship with the Hausa city-states. She established peaceful relations with these states, fostering trade and cultural exchange. This diplomatic approach not only strengthened Zazzau's position but also contributed to the overall stability and development of the region.

Legacy and Impact

QUEEN AMINA'S REIGN left an indelible mark on the history of Africa. Her military conquests expanded the borders of Zazzau, transforming it into a powerful and influential kingdom. Amina's leadership and military innovations set a precedent for future generations of female warriors, inspiring them to defy societal expectations and pursue their ambitions.

Amina's legacy extends beyond her military achievements. She is remembered as a wise and just ruler who cared deeply for her people. Her commitment to the welfare of her subjects and her efforts to promote trade and cultural exchange contributed to the prosperity of Zazzau and the surrounding regions.

Military Campaigns and Conquests

QUEEN AMINA OF ZAZZAU was not only a remarkable leader but also a formidable warrior. Her military campaigns and conquests played a significant role in shaping the history of the Zazzau Kingdom and solidifying her position as a warrior queen.

Expansion of the Zazzau Kingdom

UPON ASCENDING TO THE throne, Queen Amina wasted no time in expanding her kingdom's territory. She recognized the importance of a strong and united Zazzau Kingdom, and military conquests became the means to achieve this goal. Queen Amina led her armies on numerous campaigns, conquering neighboring territories and incorporating them into her kingdom.

Strategies and Tactics

QUEEN AMINA WAS A BRILLIANT strategist and tactician. She understood the importance of both militaries might and diplomacy in achieving her objectives. Her military campaigns were meticulously planned, and she employed various strategies to ensure victory. One of her notable tactics was the effective use of cavalry, which gave her armies a significant advantage on the battlefield. The Zazzau cavalry, led by Queen Amina herself, struck fear into the hearts of their enemies.

Conquests and Subjugation

QUEEN AMINA'S MILITARY campaigns resulted in the subjugation of numerous kingdoms and tribes. She expanded the borders of the Zazzau Kingdom, bringing under her rule territories that had previously been independent. Through a combination of military might, strategic alliances, and diplomatic negotiations, Queen Amina established herself as a dominant force in the region.

Resistance and Defeat of Enemies

QUEEN AMINA FACED NUMEROUS challenges and encountered resistance from rival kingdoms and tribes. However, her military prowess and leadership skills allowed her to overcome these obstacles. She led her armies to victory in several battles, defeating those who dared to oppose her. Queen Amina's ability to inspire loyalty and dedication among her soldiers played a crucial role in her success on the battlefield.

Legacy of Military Conquests

QUEEN AMINA'S MILITARY campaigns and conquests left a lasting impact on the Zazzau Kingdom and the surrounding regions. The territories she conquered became integral parts of her kingdom, contributing to its wealth and power. The expansion of the Zazzau Kingdom under Queen Amina's leadership brought stability and prosperity to the region.

Furthermore, Queen Amina's military successes inspired future generations of warriors and leaders. Her legacy as a warrior queen continues to be celebrated, and her military campaigns are remembered as a testament to her strength, courage, and determination. The conquests of Queen Amina of Zazzau serve as a reminder of the significant role that female warriors played in shaping the history of ancient African civilizations.

In conclusion, Queen Amina of Zazzau's military campaigns and conquests were instrumental in expanding the Zazzau Kingdom and establishing her as a formidable warrior queen. Her strategic brilliance, tactical prowess, and ability to inspire loyalty among her soldiers ensured her victories on the battlefield. The legacy of her military conquests continues to inspire and empower future generations, highlighting the important role of female warriors in African history.

Legacy and Impact

THE LEGACY AND IMPACT of Queen Amina of Zazzau are profound and far-reaching. Her reign as a warrior queen left an indelible mark on the history of Africa, particularly in the region of Zazzau (present-day Nigeria). Amina's military prowess, leadership skills, and dedication to her people have made her a legendary figure in African history.

Military Innovations

ONE OF THE MOST SIGNIFICANT aspects of Queen Amina's legacy is her military innovations. She revolutionized the tactics and strategies of warfare in the region, introducing new methods that proved highly effective in battle. Amina's army was known for its discipline, organization, and advanced weaponry, which included the use of cavalry and archers. She implemented a system of military training that ensured her soldiers were well-prepared and skilled in combat.

Amina's military innovations not only allowed her to expand her kingdom but also served as a model for future generations of African warriors. Her tactics and strategies were studied and emulated by other leaders, contributing to the development of African military traditions.

Expansion of Zazzau

UNDER QUEEN AMINA'S leadership, the kingdom of Zazzau experienced unprecedented expansion. She embarked on numerous military campaigns, conquering neighboring territories and incorporating them into her kingdom. Amina's conquests extended the influence and power of Zazzau, establishing it as a dominant force in the region.

The expansion of Zazzau under Amina's rule brought about significant economic and cultural growth. The conquered territories contributed to the wealth and prosperity of the kingdom, as they provided access to valuable resources and trade routes. Amina's reign saw the flourishing of arts, crafts, and commerce, as the kingdom became a center of cultural exchange and economic activity.

Empowerment of Women

QUEEN AMINA'S REIGN had a profound impact on the status and empowerment of women in Zazzau and beyond. As a female ruler and warrior, she shattered gender norms and challenged the prevailing patriarchal system. Amina's success as a leader and her military achievements inspired other women to defy societal expectations and pursue positions of power.

During her reign, Amina actively promoted the participation of women in various aspects of governance and warfare. She appointed women to key positions in her administration and military, recognizing their capabilities and contributions. Amina's empowerment of women created a ripple effect, encouraging the rise of other female leaders and warriors in Africa.

Cultural and Historical Significance

QUEEN AMINA'S LEGACY extends beyond her military achievements. She holds immense cultural and historical significance in African history. Amina's story has been passed down through generations, becoming a symbol of strength, courage, and resilience.

Her legacy serves as a reminder of the rich and diverse history of Africa, showcasing the power and agency of African women. Amina's story challenges the prevailing narratives that often overlook or undermine the contributions of women in shaping the continent's history.

Furthermore, Amina's legacy has inspired numerous artistic and literary works. Her story has been depicted in plays, novels, and films, further amplifying her impact and ensuring that her legacy continues to be celebrated and remembered.

Inspiration for Future Generations

QUEEN AMINA'S LEGACY continues to inspire and empower future generations of African women. Her story serves as a testament to the strength and resilience of women in the face of adversity. Amina's achievements demonstrate that women are capable of leading armies, governing kingdoms, and shaping history.

Her legacy encourages young girls and women to dream big, pursue their ambitions, and challenge societal expectations. Amina's story serves as a reminder that gender should never be a barrier to success and that women have the power to make a lasting impact on their communities and the world.

In conclusion, Queen Amina of Zazzau's legacy and impact are immeasurable. Her military innovations, expansion of Zazzau, empowerment of women, cultural significance, and inspiration for future generations have solidified her place as one of Africa's most influential warrior queens. Amina's story continues to inspire and empower, reminding us of the remarkable achievements of African women throughout history.

Queen Nzinga of Ndongo and Matamba

Background and Early Life

In order to understand the remarkable life and achievements of Queen Nzinga of Ndongo and Matamba, it is essential to delve into her background and early life. Born in 1583, Nzinga was a member of the Mbundu people, who resided in the region that is now known as Angola. She was born into the ruling family of the Ndongo kingdom, which was located in the northern part of present-day Angola.

Nzinga's early life was marked by exposure to the political and military dynamics of her kingdom. She grew up witnessing the constant struggles for power and territory between the Ndongo kingdom and the Portuguese colonizers. These experiences would shape her into the fierce and determined warrior queen that she would later become.

As a child, Nzinga was educated in the traditions and customs of her people. She was taught the importance of diplomacy, negotiation, and military strategy. These skills would prove invaluable in her later efforts to resist Portuguese colonization and defend the independence of her kingdom.

Nzinga's father, King Kiluanji, recognized her intelligence and leadership potential from an early age. He involved her in the affairs of the kingdom, allowing her to attend important meetings and discussions. This exposure to the intricacies of governance and diplomacy would lay the foundation for Nzinga's future role as a queen and stateswoman.

Tragically, Nzinga's early life was also marked by personal loss. Her father, King Kiluanji, passed away when she was just a young girl. This event thrust Nzinga into the center of a power struggle within the Ndongo kingdom. Various factions vied for control, and Nzinga's brother, Ngola Mbandi, eventually emerged as the new king.

Despite her brother's ascension to the throne, Nzinga remained a prominent figure within the kingdom. She served as an advisor to her brother and played a crucial role in shaping the policies of the Ndongo kingdom. Nzinga's intelligence, charisma, and determination earned her the respect and admiration of her people.

However, Nzinga's relationship with her brother was not without its challenges. Ngola Mbandi was a weak and indecisive ruler, often succumbing to the pressures of the Portuguese colonizers. This led to a series of devastating military defeats and the loss of significant territory to the Portuguese.

Nzinga, recognizing the dire situation facing her kingdom, took matters into her own hands. She began to form alliances with neighboring tribes and kingdoms, seeking support in her fight against the Portuguese. Nzinga's diplomatic skills and ability to forge strategic alliances would become instrumental in her later resistance efforts.

As Nzinga grew older, her influence within the Ndongo kingdom continued to grow. She became a trusted advisor to her brother, offering counsel on matters of governance and military strategy. Nzinga's reputation as a wise and capable leader spread throughout the region, earning her the respect of both her allies and adversaries.

Nzinga's early life was characterized by a unique blend of political intrigue, personal loss, and exposure to the realities of Portuguese colonization. These experiences would shape her into one of the most formidable warrior queens in African history. In the face of adversity, Nzinga's determination and resilience would propel her to become a symbol of resistance and empowerment for generations to come.

Resistance against Portuguese Colonization

QUEEN NZINGA OF NDONGO and Matamba was a remarkable warrior queen who fiercely resisted Portuguese colonization in the 17th century. Her unwavering determination and strategic brilliance made her a formidable opponent to the Portuguese forces, and her resistance efforts have left an indelible mark on African history.

Early Portuguese Encroachment

IN THE EARLY 16TH CENTURY, the Portuguese began their aggressive expansion into Africa, seeking to establish trade routes and exploit the continent's resources. They targeted the Kingdom of Ndongo, located in present-day Angola, as a prime location for their colonial ambitions. However, Queen Nzinga was not willing to surrender her kingdom to foreign invaders without a fight.

Queen Nzinga's Diplomatic Maneuvers

RECOGNIZING THE STRENGTH of the Portuguese military, Queen Nzinga employed a combination of military resistance and diplomatic negotiations to protect her people and maintain her sovereignty. She skillfully played the Portuguese against their rivals, forging alliances with other African kingdoms and European powers, such as the Dutch.

Military Strategies and Guerrilla Warfare

QUEEN NZINGA UNDERSTOOD the importance of military strategies in her resistance against the Portuguese. She organized a formidable army and implemented guerrilla warfare tactics, using the dense jungles and difficult terrain of Ndongo to her advantage. Her forces launched surprise attacks, ambushing Portuguese troops and disrupting their supply lines.

The Battle of Ngoleme

ONE OF THE MOST SIGNIFICANT battles in Queen Nzinga's resistance against Portuguese colonization was the Battle of Ngoleme in 1626. In this battle, her forces successfully repelled the Portuguese army, inflicting heavy casualties and forcing them to retreat. This victory boosted the morale of her troops and inspired other African kingdoms to join the fight against the Portuguese.

Fortifying the Kingdom of Matamba

AFTER FACING SETBACKS in Ndongo, Queen Nzinga established her base of operations in the neighboring kingdom of Matamba. Here, she continued her resistance efforts and built a formidable stronghold. She fortified the kingdom, constructing fortresses and training her army to withstand Portuguese attacks.

Queen Nzinga's Legacy

QUEEN NZINGA'S RESISTANCE against Portuguese colonization had a lasting impact on African history. Her unwavering determination and strategic brilliance inspired future generations of African leaders and freedom fighters. She became a symbol of resistance and empowerment, demonstrating that African women were capable of leading their people in times of adversity.

Influence on African Independence Movements

QUEEN NZINGA'S LEGACY extended beyond her own time. Her resistance efforts laid the groundwork for future African independence movements. Her strategies of diplomatic negotiations, military resistance, and guerrilla warfare became a blueprint for other African leaders who sought to liberate their nations from colonial rule.

Remembering Queen Nzinga

TODAY, QUEEN NZINGA is remembered as one of Africa's greatest warrior queens. Her story serves as a reminder of the strength and resilience of African women throughout history. Her resistance against Portuguese colonization stands as a testament to the indomitable spirit of African people and their determination to protect their land, culture, and sovereignty.

Lessons from Queen Nzinga's Life

QUEEN NZINGA'S LIFE offers valuable lessons for contemporary society. Her ability to navigate complex political landscapes, forge alliances, and lead her people in times of crisis showcases the importance of strategic thinking and resilience. Her story also highlights the significant contributions of African women in shaping history and fighting for justice and equality.

Continuing the Legacy of Female Empowerment

QUEEN NZINGA'S LEGACY serves as a powerful inspiration for women around the world. Her story encourages women to embrace their strength, intelligence, and leadership abilities. It reminds us that women have always played a vital role in shaping societies and that their contributions should be recognized and celebrated.

In the face of Portuguese colonization, Queen Nzinga stood as a beacon of resistance and resilience. Her unwavering determination and strategic brilliance continue to inspire generations, reminding us of the indomitable spirit of African women and their crucial role in shaping history.

Diplomacy and Military Strategies

DIPLOMACY AND MILITARY strategies played a crucial role in the success of African warrior queens. These remarkable women not only possessed exceptional leadership skills but also demonstrated a deep understanding of diplomacy and military tactics. Through their strategic thinking and diplomatic prowess, they were able to navigate complex political landscapes, forge alliances, and effectively lead their armies to victory.

Diplomacy: Building Alliances and Negotiating Peace

AFRICAN WARRIOR QUEENS recognized the importance of diplomacy in achieving their goals. They understood that building alliances with neighboring kingdoms and tribes could strengthen their military forces and provide them with crucial support. These queens were skilled negotiators, adept at forging alliances through marriage alliances, trade agreements, and political alliances.

Queen Nzinga of Ndongo and Matamba, for example, was a master diplomat. She skillfully navigated the political landscape of 17th-century Central Africa, forging alliances with various African states and European powers. Nzinga understood the power of diplomacy in her fight against Portuguese colonization. She formed alliances with the Dutch and the Kingdom of Kongo, leveraging their support to resist Portuguese encroachment.

Similarly, Queen Amanirenas of Kush employed diplomacy to negotiate a peace treaty with the Roman Empire. After leading a successful military campaign against the Romans, Amanirenas recognized the need for a diplomatic solution to ensure the long-term stability of her kingdom. Through negotiations, she secured favorable terms, including the withdrawal of Roman forces from Kushite territory.

Military Strategies: Adaptability and Innovation

AFRICAN WARRIOR QUEENS were not only skilled diplomats but also brilliant military strategists. They understood the importance of adapting their tactics to the specific terrain, resources, and strengths of their armies. These queens employed a range of military strategies, including guerrilla warfare, defensive tactics, and surprise attacks, to outmaneuver their enemies and secure victory.

Queen Yaa Asantewaa of the Ashanti Empire, for instance, employed innovative military strategies during the Ashanti resistance against British colonialism. Recognizing the superior firepower of the British forces, Yaa Asantewaa organized her troops into smaller, more agile units, allowing them to launch surprise attacks and retreat quickly. This guerrilla warfare tactic proved highly effective in countering the British forces and prolonging the resistance.

Queen Ranavalona I of Madagascar also demonstrated exceptional military strategies during her reign. She implemented a policy of isolationism, fortifying the island and adopting defensive tactics to protect her kingdom from European colonization. Ranavalona's military strategies, combined with her strict policies against foreign influence, allowed her to maintain the independence of Madagascar throughout her reign.

Psychological Warfare: Inspiring Loyalty and Fear

IN ADDITION TO DIPLOMATIC negotiations and military tactics, African warrior queens understood the power of psychological warfare. They employed various strategies to inspire loyalty among their troops and strike fear into the hearts of their enemies. These queens utilized symbols, rituals, and storytelling to create a sense of unity and purpose among their armies.

Queen Nandi of the Zulu Kingdom, for example, played a crucial role in shaping the military culture of the Zulu people. She instilled a sense of discipline, bravery, and loyalty in her son, Shaka Zulu, who would go on to become one of Africa's greatest military leaders. Nandi's influence on the Zulu military tactics and her ability to inspire loyalty among her people contributed significantly to the success of the Zulu Kingdom.

Queen Kahina of the Berber Kingdom also employed psychological warfare to great effect. She used her reputation as a powerful sorceress and her ability to communicate with the spirits to strike fear into the hearts of her enemies. This psychological advantage, combined with her military strategies, allowed Kahina to successfully resist the Arab conquest for several years.

In conclusion, African warrior queens were not only fierce warriors but also skilled diplomats and military strategists. Their ability to navigate complex political landscapes, forge alliances, and employ innovative military tactics played a crucial role in their success. Through diplomacy, adaptability, and psychological warfare, these remarkable women left a lasting legacy and continue to inspire generations of female empowerment.

Legacy and Influence

THE LEGACY AND INFLUENCE of Queen Nzinga of Ndongo and Matamba are profound and far-reaching. Her remarkable leadership, diplomatic skills, and military strategies have left an indelible mark on African history and continue to inspire generations of women across the continent.

Inspiring African Women

QUEEN NZINGA'S STORY serves as a powerful inspiration for African women, demonstrating their strength, resilience, and ability to challenge societal norms. Her unwavering determination to protect her people and resist Portuguese colonization has become a symbol of female empowerment and resistance.

Challenging Gender Roles

QUEEN NZINGA'S REIGN challenged traditional gender roles and shattered the notion that women were incapable of leading nations or engaging in warfare. By assuming the role of a warrior queen, she defied societal expectations and proved that women were just as capable as men in matters of governance and military strategy.

Diplomatic Prowess

ONE OF QUEEN NZINGA'S most significant contributions was her exceptional diplomatic skills. She engaged in negotiations with the Portuguese colonizers, skillfully playing the political game to protect her people's interests. Her ability to navigate complex diplomatic situations and forge alliances with neighboring tribes showcased her astuteness and strategic thinking.

Military Strategies

QUEEN NZINGA'S MILITARY strategies were innovative and effective, enabling her to resist Portuguese aggression for many years. She employed guerrilla warfare tactics, utilizing the difficult terrain of Ndongo and Matamba to her advantage. Her ability to mobilize and lead her troops in battle demonstrated her military prowess and tactical brilliance.

Legacy in Angola

QUEEN NZINGA'S LEGACY in Angola is profound. Her resistance against Portuguese colonization inspired future generations of Angolan freedom fighters and nationalists. Her story continues to be celebrated in Angola, with statues, monuments, and street names dedicated to her memory. Queen Nzinga's legacy serves as a reminder of the strength and resilience of the Angolan people.

Influence on African Independence Movements

QUEEN NZINGA'S LEGACY extends beyond Angola and has had a significant impact on African independence movements. Her story has served as a source of inspiration for leaders such as Patrice Lumumba, Amílcar Cabral, and Agostinho Neto, who fought for the liberation of their respective countries. Queen Nzinga's courage and determination have become a symbol of African resistance against colonialism and oppression.

Empowering Women's Rights Movements

QUEEN NZINGA'S STORY has also played a crucial role in empowering women's rights movements across Africa. Her defiance of gender norms and her ability to lead in a male-dominated society have become a rallying cry for women seeking equality and recognition. Queen Nzinga's legacy has inspired countless African women to challenge societal expectations and pursue leadership roles in various fields.

Cultural Impact

QUEEN NZINGA'S CULTURAL impact is evident in various aspects of Angolan society. Her story has been immortalized in literature, music, and art, with numerous books, songs, and paintings dedicated to her memory. She has become a symbol of national pride and identity, representing the strength and resilience of the Angolan people.

International Recognition

QUEEN NZINGA'S REMARKABLE achievements have gained international recognition and admiration. Her story has been shared and celebrated worldwide, contributing to a broader understanding of African history and the significant role played by women in shaping it. Queen Nzinga's legacy serves as a testament to the strength and leadership capabilities of African women throughout history.

Continuing the Legacy

THE LEGACY OF QUEEN Nzinga serves as a call to action for future generations to continue the fight for equality, justice, and empowerment. Her story reminds us of the importance of challenging societal norms, advocating for the rights of marginalized communities, and standing up against oppression. By embracing Queen Nzinga's legacy, African women can find inspiration and strength to overcome obstacles and make their mark on history.

In conclusion, Queen Nzinga's legacy and influence are immeasurable. Her remarkable leadership, diplomatic prowess, and military strategies have left an indelible mark on African history. Her story continues to inspire and empower women across the continent, challenging gender roles and advocating for equality. Queen Nzinga's cultural impact and international recognition further solidify her place as one of Africa's most influential warrior queens. Her legacy serves as a reminder of the strength, resilience, and leadership capabilities of African women throughout history, inspiring future generations to continue the fight for empowerment and equality.

Queen Yaa Asentewaa of Ashanti Empire

The Ashanti Empire and British Colonialism

The Ashanti Empire, also known as the Asante Empire, was a powerful and influential kingdom in West Africa during the 18th and 19th centuries. Located in what is now modern-day Ghana, the Ashanti Empire was renowned for its military prowess, rich cultural heritage, and strong political organization. However, the empire's existence was not without its challenges, particularly when it came face to face with the forces of British colonialism.

The Rise of the Ashanti Empire

THE ASHANTI EMPIRE emerged in the late 17th century under the leadership of Osei Tutu, who united several Akan states to form a centralized and powerful kingdom. The empire quickly expanded its influence through military conquests and strategic alliances, establishing itself as a dominant force in the region. The Ashanti people, known for their skilled warriors and sophisticated administrative systems, built a prosperous empire based on trade, agriculture, and gold mining.

British Colonial Ambitions

AS EUROPEAN POWERS began to explore and exploit Africa, the British Empire set its sights on the rich resources and trade opportunities offered by the Ashanti Empire. The British were particularly interested in the region's abundant reserves of gold and the lucrative slave trade. They saw the Ashanti Empire as a potential obstacle to their ambitions and sought to establish control over the region.

The First Anglo-Ashanti War

TENSIONS BETWEEN THE Ashanti Empire and the British Empire escalated in the early 19th century, leading to the outbreak of the First Anglo-Ashanti War in 1823. The Ashanti, under the leadership of King Osei Bonsu, fiercely resisted British attempts to encroach upon their territory. The war was marked by several battles, with both sides experiencing victories and defeats. However, the Ashanti ultimately managed to repel the British forces and maintain their independence.

The Ashanti-British Conflict Intensifies

FOLLOWING THE FIRST Anglo-Ashanti War, the Ashanti Empire continued to resist British encroachment. The British, determined to assert their dominance, launched a series of military campaigns against the Ashanti. These conflicts, known as the Ashanti-British Wars, spanned several decades and were characterized by fierce resistance from the Ashanti warriors.

Yaa Asantewaa's Call to Arms

IN THE LATE 19TH CENTURY, the Ashanti Empire faced a critical moment in its history. The British, seeking to exploit the region's resources, demanded the Golden Stool, a sacred symbol of Ashanti unity and sovereignty. In response to this affront, Queen Mother Yaa Asantewaa emerged as a powerful leader and advocate for Ashanti independence.

Yaa Asantewaa, a respected queen mother and member of the Ashanti royal family, rallied the Ashanti people to resist British colonialism. In 1900, she delivered a powerful speech, urging the Ashanti warriors to take up arms and defend their land. Her call to arms galvanized the Ashanti people, both men and women, to fight against the British forces.

The Battle of Ejisu

THE BATTLE OF EJISU, which took place in March 1900, was a pivotal moment in the Ashanti-British conflict. Yaa Asantewaa led an army of Ashanti warriors, including many brave and skilled women, into battle against the British forces. Despite being outnumbered and outgunned, the Ashanti fought valiantly, displaying their military prowess and determination.

Although the Ashanti forces were ultimately defeated, the Battle of Ejisu showcased the resilience and bravery of the Ashanti warriors, particularly the women who fought alongside their male counterparts. Yaa Asantewaa's leadership and the participation of women in the battle challenged traditional gender roles and demonstrated the strength and courage of African women in the face of colonial oppression.

Aftermath and Legacy

FOLLOWING THE DEFEAT at the Battle of Ejisu, the Ashanti Empire was formally incorporated into the British Gold Coast colony in 1902. However, the resistance and legacy of Yaa Asantewaa and the Ashanti warriors left an indelible mark on the history of the Ashanti people and the broader struggle against colonialism in Africa.

Yaa Asantewaa's leadership and the participation of women in the Ashanti-British conflict challenged prevailing notions of gender roles and highlighted the important role that women played in African societies. Her bravery and determination continue to inspire generations of women in Ghana and beyond, serving as a reminder of the strength and resilience of African warrior queens.

In conclusion, the Ashanti Empire's encounter with British colonialism was a significant chapter in African history. The resistance led by Yaa Asantewaa and the Ashanti warriors demonstrated the unwavering spirit of the Ashanti people in the face of oppression. Their story serves as a testament to the power and influence of female warriors in shaping the course of African history.

Yaa Asantewaa's Leadership and Resistance

YAA ASANTEWAA, ALSO known as Nana Yaa Asantewaa, was a remarkable warrior queen from the Ashanti Empire in present-day Ghana. Her leadership and resistance against British colonialism made her a symbol of courage and strength in African history. Yaa Asantewaa's story is a testament to the power of female leadership and the determination to fight for freedom and independence.

Early Life and Background

YAA ASANTEWAA WAS BORN in 1840 in Besease, a small village in the Ashanti Empire. She was a member of the royal family and grew up with a deep understanding of Ashanti traditions and customs. As a young girl, she witnessed the power and influence of her mother, who was a respected queen mother in the empire. This upbringing instilled in Yaa Asantewaa a sense of pride in her heritage and a strong belief in the importance of defending her people.

The Ashanti Empire and British Colonialism

DURING THE LATE 19TH century, the Ashanti Empire faced increasing threats from European powers, particularly the British. The empire, known for its rich resources and strong military, became a target for colonization. The British aimed to exploit the empire's gold mines and establish control over the region. They employed various tactics, including diplomacy, economic manipulation, and military force, to achieve their goals.

Yaa Asantewaa's Leadership and Resistance

IN 1900, THE ASHANTI Empire faced a critical moment when the British exiled the Ashanti king, Prempeh I, and attempted to seize the Golden Stool, a symbol of Ashanti unity and sovereignty. This act of aggression sparked outrage among the Ashanti people, and Yaa Asantewaa emerged as a prominent leader in the resistance movement.

Yaa Asantewaa recognized the urgency of the situation and the need for decisive action. She rallied the Ashanti people, particularly the women, to take up arms and defend their land. Her powerful speeches and charismatic leadership inspired thousands to join the fight against the British colonial forces.

The Battle of Ejisu and Aftermath

UNDER YAA ASANTEWAA'S leadership, the Ashanti forces engaged in a fierce battle against the British at Ejisu, a town in the Ashanti region. Despite being outnumbered and outgunned, the Ashanti warriors fought valiantly, displaying their unwavering determination to protect their homeland.

Although the Ashanti forces were ultimately defeated in the Battle of Ejisu, Yaa Asantewaa's resistance had a profound impact on the Ashanti people and the broader African community. Her bravery and leadership inspired a sense of unity and defiance against colonial oppression.

Remembering Yaa Asantewaa

YAA ASANTEWAA'S LEGACY continues to resonate in Ghana and beyond. Her courageous stand against British colonialism has made her an iconic figure in African history. Her name is celebrated in songs, poems, and stories, ensuring that her story is passed down through generations.

In Ghana, Yaa Asantewaa Day is celebrated annually on August 1st to honor her memory and recognize her contributions to the fight for independence. The day serves as a reminder of the importance of female leadership and the ongoing struggle for freedom and equality.

Yaa Asantewaa's leadership and resistance serve as a powerful example of the significant role that women played in African history. Her determination to protect her people and her unwavering commitment to the cause of freedom have made her an inspiration for women across the continent.

Conclusion

THE STORIES OF WARRIOR queens like Yaa Asantewaa highlight the significant contributions of women in African history. These remarkable leaders defied societal norms and fought against oppression, leaving a lasting impact on their communities and inspiring future generations.

The lives of warrior queens teach us valuable lessons about courage, resilience, and the power of unity. Their stories remind us of the importance of recognizing and celebrating the achievements of women in history. By continuing their legacy of female empowerment, we can strive for a more inclusive and equal society.

The Battle of Ejisu and Aftermath

THE BATTLE OF EJISU was a pivotal moment in the life of Queen Yaa Asantewaa of the Ashanti Empire. It was a fierce conflict that showcased her leadership, bravery, and determination to protect her people from British colonial rule. This battle not only marked a significant event in the history of the Ashanti Empire but also solidified Queen Yaa Asantewaa's place as one of Africa's most revered warrior queens.

The Prelude to Battle

THE ASHANTI EMPIRE, located in present-day Ghana, was a powerful and prosperous kingdom in the late 19th century. However, the empire faced the threat of British colonization, as the British sought to expand their influence and control over the region. The Ashanti people, led by their king, Prempeh I, resisted British encroachment, but their efforts were met with aggression and attempts to undermine their authority.

In 1896, the British governor, Sir Frederick Hodgson, demanded the Golden Stool, a sacred symbol of Ashanti unity and sovereignty. This act of disrespect and disregard for Ashanti traditions and beliefs sparked outrage among the Ashanti people. It was in this volatile atmosphere that Queen Yaa Asantewaa emerged as a formidable leader and advocate for her people's rights.

The Call to Arms

QUEEN YAA ASANTEWAA, known for her wisdom and courage, rallied the Ashanti people to resist British oppression. She called upon the men and women of the empire to take up arms and defend their land, their traditions, and their freedom. Queen Yaa Asantewaa's call to arms was met with overwhelming support, and an army of thousands gathered to fight for their independence.

The Battle of Ejisu

THE BATTLE OF EJISU took place in March 1900, near the town of Ejisu in the Ashanti Empire. Queen Yaa Asantewaa led her army into battle against the British forces, displaying exceptional military strategy and bravery. The Ashanti warriors fought fiercely, using their knowledge of the terrain and their determination to protect their homeland.

The battle was intense and lasted for several days. Queen Yaa Asantewaa's forces employed guerrilla tactics, ambushing the British troops and inflicting heavy casualties. Despite being outnumbered and outgunned, the Ashanti warriors displayed remarkable resilience and courage.

The Aftermath

ALTHOUGH THE ASHANTI forces fought valiantly, they were eventually overwhelmed by the superior firepower of the British. The Battle of Ejisu ended in defeat for the Ashanti Empire, and Queen Yaa Asantewaa and her remaining forces were forced to retreat. However, the battle had a profound impact on the Ashanti people and their struggle for independence.

Queen Yaa Asantewaa's leadership and bravery inspired a sense of unity and resilience among the Ashanti people. Her unwavering determination to fight for their freedom became a symbol of resistance against British colonialism. The Battle of Ejisu served as a catalyst for further resistance and fueled the Ashanti people's desire to regain their independence.

The Legacy of Queen Yaa Asantewaa

QUEEN YAA ASANTEWAA'S legacy extends far beyond the Battle of Ejisu. Her courageous stand against British oppression and her unwavering commitment to her people's rights have made her an iconic figure in African history. She is remembered as a symbol of female empowerment, leadership, and resistance.

Queen Yaa Asantewaa's legacy continues to inspire women across Africa and the world. Her story serves as a reminder of the strength and resilience of African women and their significant contributions to the fight for freedom and equality. Today, Queen Yaa Asantewaa is celebrated as a national hero in Ghana, and her legacy lives on in the hearts and minds of those who continue to fight for justice and empowerment.

In conclusion, the Battle of Ejisu was a defining moment in the life of Queen Yaa Asantewaa and the Ashanti Empire. It showcased her leadership, bravery, and determination to protect her people from British colonial rule. Despite the ultimate defeat, the battle left a lasting impact on the Ashanti people's struggle for independence and solidified Queen Yaa Asantewaa's place as a revered warrior queen in African history. Her legacy continues to inspire and empower women to this day, reminding us of the importance of female leadership and the ongoing fight for equality.

Remembering Yaa Asantewaa

YAA ASANTEWAA, THE fearless warrior queen of the Ashanti Empire, left an indelible mark on African history through her leadership and resistance against British colonialism. Her unwavering determination and bravery continue to inspire generations of women in Africa and beyond. In this section, we will delve into the life and legacy of Yaa Asantewaa, highlighting her remarkable contributions to the fight for freedom and the empowerment of women.

Early Life and Background

YAA ASANTEWAA WAS BORN in 1840 in Besease, a small village in what is now modern-day Ghana. She was a member of the Ashanti ethnic group, which was known for its rich cultural heritage and strong warrior traditions. From a young age, Yaa Asantewaa was exposed to the stories and legends of her ancestors, who had fought valiantly to protect their land and people.

The Ashanti Empire and British Colonialism

DURING THE 19TH CENTURY, the Ashanti Empire faced increasing threats from European powers, particularly the British, who sought to expand their colonial territories in West Africa. The Ashanti people fiercely resisted these encroachments, but by the late 1800s, the British had gained significant control over the region.

Yaa Asantewaa's Leadership and Resistance

IN 1900, THE ASHANTI king, Prempeh I, was exiled by the British, leaving a power vacuum in the empire. Yaa Asantewaa, recognizing the urgent need for action, emerged as a prominent leader and rallied the Ashanti people to resist British oppression. She passionately addressed the Ashanti chiefs and warriors, urging them to unite and fight for their freedom.

Yaa Asantewaa's leadership was characterized by her unwavering commitment to the cause and her ability to inspire others. She organized an army of thousands, both men and women, and led them into battle against the British. Her strategic prowess and tactical skills were evident as she devised effective military strategies to counter the British forces.

The Battle of Ejisu and Aftermath

THE MOST SIGNIFICANT battle led by Yaa Asantewaa was the Battle of Ejisu in March 1900. The Ashanti forces, under her command, engaged in fierce combat with the British troops. Despite being outnumbered and outgunned, Yaa Asantewaa's army fought valiantly, displaying immense courage and resilience.

Although the Ashanti forces were ultimately defeated in the Battle of Ejisu, Yaa Asantewaa's resistance had a profound impact on the Ashanti people and the wider African community. Her bravery and determination inspired others to continue the fight for independence and galvanized the spirit of resistance against colonial rule.

Legacy and Cultural Significance

YAA ASANTEWAA'S LEGACY extends far beyond her military achievements. She became a symbol of strength, courage, and female empowerment in Africa. Her leadership challenged traditional gender roles and shattered the notion that women were incapable of leading in times of crisis.

Yaa Asantewaa's resistance against British colonialism also had a lasting impact on the Ashanti Empire. Her actions sparked a renewed sense of national pride and unity among the Ashanti people, fostering a spirit of resilience that would endure for generations to come.

Today, Yaa Asantewaa is celebrated as a national hero in Ghana. Her legacy is honored through various means, including statues, monuments, and the annual Yaa Asantewaa Festival, which commemorates her bravery and leadership. Her story continues to inspire women across Africa and serves as a reminder of the power of determination and the ability to effect change.

Continuing the Legacy of Female Empowerment

THE LEGACY OF YAA ASANTEWAA and other warrior queens in Africa serves as a powerful reminder of the significant contributions women have made throughout history. Their stories challenge societal norms and inspire women to break barriers and pursue their dreams fearlessly.

In contemporary Africa, the fight for gender equality and female empowerment continues. Women are actively engaged in various fields, including politics, education, and entrepreneurship, striving to create a more inclusive and equitable society. The spirit of Yaa Asantewaa lives on in these women, who draw strength from her example and work towards a future where women's voices are heard and their contributions valued.

As we remember Yaa Asantewaa and her remarkable achievements, let us also recognize the countless other warrior queens who have left an indelible mark on African history. Their stories deserve to be told, celebrated, and passed down to future generations, inspiring them to embrace their own power and potential.

Queen Makeda of Sheba

The Legend of Queen Makeda

Queen Makeda, also known as the Queen of Sheba, is a legendary figure in African history and folklore. Her story has captivated the imaginations of people for centuries, and her legacy continues to inspire and intrigue to this day. The tale of Queen Makeda is steeped in mystery, romance, and power, making her one of the most iconic warrior queens in African history.

According to the legend, Queen Makeda ruled over the ancient kingdom of Sheba, which was located in what is now modern-day Ethiopia and Yemen. She was renowned for her beauty, wisdom, and wealth, which attracted the attention of King Solomon of Israel. The story of their meeting and the subsequent romance between the two rulers has been passed down through generations.

The legend tells of Queen Makeda's journey to Jerusalem to meet King Solomon, drawn by his fame and wisdom. She arrived at his court with a grand entourage, bringing with her precious gifts and spices from her kingdom. The meeting between the two rulers was said to be a meeting of equals, with both displaying their intelligence and wit in a series of intellectual exchanges.

The legend goes on to describe the deep connection that developed between Queen Makeda and King Solomon during her stay in Jerusalem. They shared knowledge, ideas, and cultural practices, and it is believed that their relationship extended beyond the intellectual realm. Some versions of the legend even suggest that Queen Makeda bore King

Solomon a son, Menelik, who would go on to become the first emperor of Ethiopia.

The story of Queen Makeda and King Solomon is not only a tale of romance but also one of power and influence. Queen Makeda was a formidable ruler in her own right, known for her strategic thinking and diplomatic skills. She was respected by her subjects and feared by her enemies, and her kingdom flourished under her rule.

Queen Makeda's legacy extends far beyond her romantic encounter with King Solomon. She is revered as a symbol of African power and independence, and her story has become intertwined with the history and culture of Ethiopia. The Ethiopian Orthodox Church even claims to possess the Ark of the Covenant, which is said to have been brought to Ethiopia by Queen Makeda.

In addition to her political and cultural impact, Queen Makeda's story has also had a profound influence on literature, art, and music. Her tale has been retold in various forms, from ancient texts to modern novels and films. Artists and musicians have been inspired by her beauty and strength, creating works that celebrate her legacy.

The legend of Queen Makeda continues to capture the imagination of people around the world. Her story serves as a reminder of the power and resilience of African women throughout history. Queen Makeda's journey to Jerusalem and her encounter with King Solomon symbolize the strength and determination of African queens who defied societal norms and carved their own paths.

While the legend of Queen Makeda may be shrouded in myth and folklore, her impact on African history and culture is undeniable. She remains an iconic figure, representing the strength, intelligence, and beauty of African women. Queen Makeda's story serves as an inspiration for women everywhere, reminding them of their own potential to lead, conquer, and shape the world around them.

Meeting with King Solomon

QUEEN MAKEDA, ALSO known as the Queen of Sheba, is a legendary figure in African history. Her story is shrouded in mystery and has been passed down through generations. According to the legends, Queen Makeda was a powerful and wise ruler who reigned over the ancient kingdom of Sheba, located in present-day Ethiopia and Yemen.

The meeting between Queen Makeda and King Solomon of Israel is one of the most famous stories associated with her. It is said that Queen Makeda had heard of King Solomon's great wisdom and wanted to test his knowledge for herself. She embarked on a long and arduous journey to Jerusalem, bringing with her a caravan of precious gifts and spices.

When Queen Makeda arrived in Jerusalem, she was greeted with great honor and respect by King Solomon. The meeting between the two rulers was a meeting of minds, as they engaged in deep conversations about philosophy, religion, and governance. Queen Makeda was impressed by King Solomon's wisdom and was captivated by his charm and intelligence.

During their time together, Queen Makeda and King Solomon exchanged not only knowledge but also gifts. Queen Makeda presented King Solomon with rare and valuable treasures from her kingdom, including gold, precious stones, and exotic spices. In return, King Solomon bestowed upon Queen Makeda gifts of equal grandeur, including fine fabrics, luxurious perfumes, and exquisite jewelry.

The meeting between Queen Makeda and King Solomon was not only a meeting of two powerful rulers but also a meeting of two great civilizations. It was a cultural exchange that allowed both leaders to gain a deeper understanding of each other's customs, traditions, and beliefs. This meeting laid the foundation for future trade and diplomatic relations between the Kingdom of Sheba and the Kingdom of Israel.

The Wisdom of King Solomon

ONE OF THE MOST SIGNIFICANT aspects of the meeting between Queen Makeda and King Solomon was the exchange of wisdom. King Solomon was renowned for his wisdom and was known for his ability to solve complex problems and dilemmas. Queen Makeda, too, was a wise and intelligent ruler, and their discussions were filled with intellectual depth and insight.

King Solomon shared his knowledge of governance, justice, and the arts with Queen Makeda. He spoke of his experiences in ruling a vast kingdom and imparted his wisdom on matters of statecraft and diplomacy. Queen Makeda, in turn, shared her knowledge of the rich cultural heritage of the Kingdom of Sheba, including its traditions, customs, and spiritual beliefs.

The wisdom shared between Queen Makeda and King Solomon went beyond mere intellectual discourse. It was a meeting of minds that allowed both leaders to gain a deeper understanding of the world and their respective roles as rulers. They discussed the importance of justice, compassion, and the well-being of their people. Their conversations were not only enlightening but also inspiring, as they sought to create a better future for their kingdoms.

The Romance Between Queen Makeda and King Solomon

THE MEETING BETWEEN Queen Makeda and King Solomon was not only a meeting of minds but also a meeting of hearts. According to some legends, Queen Makeda and King Solomon developed a deep and passionate love for each other during their time together. Their connection went beyond the realms of politics and diplomacy, transcending into a romantic relationship.

The romance between Queen Makeda and King Solomon is often depicted as a tale of love and longing. It is said that Queen Makeda was captivated by King Solomon's wisdom, charm, and physical beauty. King

Solomon, too, was enamored by Queen Makeda's intelligence, grace, and regal presence. Their love for each other was said to be intense and profound, transcending the boundaries of their respective kingdoms.

However, the romance between Queen Makeda and King Solomon was not without its challenges. The distance between their kingdoms and the responsibilities they held as rulers made it difficult for them to be together. Despite their deep love for each other, they had to part ways, with Queen Makeda returning to her kingdom of Sheba.

The Legacy of Queen Makeda and King Solomon

THE MEETING BETWEEN Queen Makeda and King Solomon left a lasting impact on both their kingdoms and the world at large. It solidified the diplomatic and trade relations between the Kingdom of Sheba and the Kingdom of Israel, leading to a flourishing exchange of goods, ideas, and culture.

Queen Makeda's journey to Jerusalem and her meeting with King Solomon became the stuff of legends, inspiring countless stories, poems, and songs throughout the ages. The tale of their romance has been immortalized in literature and art, symbolizing the power of love and the meeting of two great civilizations.

The legacy of Queen Makeda and King Solomon extends beyond their individual reigns. Their meeting represents the potential for understanding, cooperation, and unity between different cultures and nations. It serves as a reminder that wisdom, love, and diplomacy can bridge the gaps between people and create a better world.

In conclusion, the meeting between Queen Makeda and King Solomon was a momentous event in African history. It brought together two powerful rulers, allowing them to exchange wisdom, knowledge, and love. Their meeting left a lasting impact on their kingdoms and continues to inspire generations with its message of unity and understanding. Queen Makeda and King Solomon's story is a testament to the enduring power of female warriors and their ability to shape history.

Legacy and Cultural Impact

THE LEGACY OF QUEEN Makeda of Sheba, also known as the Queen of Sheba, has had a profound cultural impact on Africa and beyond. Her story, as depicted in various ancient texts and oral traditions, has captivated the imaginations of people for centuries. The tale of her journey to meet King Solomon of Israel and their subsequent romance has become a symbol of power, wisdom, and cultural exchange.

Cultural Significance

QUEEN MAKEDA'S STORY holds immense cultural significance, particularly in Ethiopia and other parts of Africa. She is considered a legendary figure and an important part of Ethiopian history and identity. The Ethiopian Orthodox Church recognizes her as a saint, and her lineage is believed to have continued through the Solomonic dynasty, which ruled Ethiopia for centuries.

The legend of Queen Makeda has also influenced various aspects of Ethiopian culture. It has inspired numerous works of art, including paintings, sculptures, and literature. Ethiopian music and dance often incorporate elements of her story, celebrating her beauty, intelligence, and strength. The tale of her encounter with King Solomon has been reimagined in plays, operas, and films, further cementing her place in popular culture.

Trade and Cultural Exchange

QUEEN MAKEDA'S MEETING with King Solomon is often seen as a symbol of trade and cultural exchange between ancient African civilizations and the rest of the world. According to the legend, she brought gifts of gold, spices, and precious stones to the king, showcasing the wealth and prosperity of her kingdom. This exchange of goods and ideas played a significant role in shaping the cultural landscape of the time.

The story of Queen Makeda and King Solomon also highlights the importance of diplomacy and peaceful relations between nations. Their meeting was not only a romantic encounter but also a diplomatic mission aimed at establishing friendly ties and fostering mutual respect. This aspect of the story continues to resonate with people today, emphasizing the value of diplomacy and cultural understanding in building strong relationships between nations.

Women's Empowerment

QUEEN MAKEDA'S STORY has become a symbol of women's empowerment and leadership. As a powerful queen who ruled over a prosperous kingdom, she defied traditional gender roles and expectations. Her journey to meet King Solomon showcased her independence, intelligence, and determination. Queen Makeda's story has inspired generations of women to pursue their dreams, break barriers, and assert their rightful place in society.

In Ethiopia, Queen Makeda is often seen as a role model for women in positions of power. Her story serves as a reminder that women are capable of ruling with wisdom and strength. Her legacy has contributed to the empowerment of women in Ethiopia and beyond, inspiring them to take on leadership roles and make a positive impact in their communities.

Symbol of African Identity

QUEEN MAKEDA'S STORY has also become a symbol of African identity and pride. Her encounter with King Solomon is seen as a testament to the rich history and cultural heritage of Africa. The legend highlights the achievements and contributions of ancient African civilizations, challenging the notion that Africa was solely a recipient of foreign influence.

By celebrating Queen Makeda's story, Africans assert their agency and reclaim their narrative. It serves as a reminder of the greatness that existed within their own societies long before the arrival of colonial powers. Queen Makeda's legacy has become an integral part of the African cultural tapestry, reinforcing a sense of pride and unity among Africans worldwide.

Inspiration for Future Generations

THE STORY OF QUEEN Makeda continues to inspire future generations to embrace their heritage, pursue knowledge, and strive for greatness. Her journey to meet King Solomon exemplifies the importance of curiosity, exploration, and the pursuit of wisdom. It encourages individuals to seek knowledge beyond their own borders and engage in cultural exchange.

Queen Makeda's legacy also serves as a reminder that women have played significant roles in shaping history, even in male-dominated societies. Her story challenges gender stereotypes and encourages young girls to dream big, pursue their passions, and overcome societal barriers.

In conclusion, the legacy of Queen Makeda of Sheba has had a profound cultural impact on Africa and beyond. Her story has become a symbol of power, wisdom, and cultural exchange. It has influenced Ethiopian culture, inspired trade and diplomatic relations, empowered women, and become a symbol of African identity. Queen Makeda's story continues to inspire future

Queen Ranavalona I of Madagascar

Rise to Power and Early Reign

Queen Ranavalona I of Madagascar was a formidable ruler who rose to power in the early 19th century. Born as Princess Ramavo, she belonged to the Merina ethnic group, which was one of the dominant groups in Madagascar at the time. Ranavalona's ascent to the throne was not a straightforward one, as she faced numerous challenges and power struggles within the royal court.

Ranavalona's father, King Andrianampoinimerina, had multiple wives and many children. However, it was Ranavalona's intelligence, determination, and political acumen that set her apart from her siblings. She quickly gained the favor of her father, who recognized her potential as a future leader. This favoritism, however, created resentment among her siblings and other members of the royal court.

When King Andrianampoinimerina passed away in 1810, a power struggle ensued among his children to claim the throne. Ranavalona's older brother, Radama I, initially ascended to power. However, his reign was short-lived, as he died under mysterious circumstances in 1828. This event opened the door for Ranavalona to seize the throne and become the first female sovereign of Madagascar.

Ranavalona's early reign was marked by a series of challenges and threats to her authority. Many members of the royal court, particularly the nobles who had supported her brother, were skeptical of her ability to rule effectively. Additionally, there were external pressures from

European powers, particularly France and Britain, who sought to exert their influence over the island.

To consolidate her power, Ranavalona took decisive actions to eliminate potential threats and assert her authority. She purged the court of her brother's loyalists and established a network of spies to monitor any dissent or opposition. She also implemented strict laws and regulations to maintain control over the kingdom.

One of the key aspects of Ranavalona's early reign was her focus on military policies. Recognizing the need to defend Madagascar from external threats, she prioritized the strengthening of the kingdom's military capabilities. She expanded the army, modernized weaponry, and implemented rigorous training programs for her soldiers.

Ranavalona's military policies were not solely defensive in nature. She also sought to expand her influence and control over neighboring territories. Through a series of military campaigns, she successfully annexed several regions and brought them under her rule. These conquests not only expanded the borders of her kingdom but also solidified her position as a powerful and respected ruler.

However, Ranavalona's reign was not without controversy. She implemented a policy of isolationism, cutting off contact with European powers and expelling Christian missionaries from the island. This decision was driven by a desire to preserve Madagascar's cultural and religious traditions, which she believed were under threat from foreign influences.

The persecution of Christians during Ranavalona's reign was severe and brutal. Missionaries and converts were subjected to torture, imprisonment, and execution. This policy, known as the "Madagascar Martyrs," resulted in the deaths of thousands of people and created a lasting legacy of religious persecution.

Despite the controversy surrounding her reign, Ranavalona's early years in power were marked by stability and territorial expansion. She successfully navigated the complex political landscape of Madagascar and established herself as a formidable leader. Her military policies and determination to protect the kingdom from external threats laid the foundation for a reign that would shape the history of Madagascar.

In the next section, we will explore Ranavalona's consolidation of power and the military policies she implemented to maintain her authority.

Consolidation of Power and Military Policies

AFTER QUEEN RANAVALONA I ascended to the throne of Madagascar, she faced numerous challenges in consolidating her power and establishing her authority over the kingdom. With a strong determination and a strategic mindset, she implemented various military policies that not only solidified her rule but also ensured the protection and stability of her kingdom.

Strengthening the Military

ONE OF QUEEN RANAVALONA I's first priorities was to strengthen the military forces of Madagascar. She recognized the importance of a well-trained and disciplined army to defend her kingdom against external threats and maintain internal order. To achieve this, she implemented rigorous training programs for her soldiers, focusing on physical fitness, combat skills, and tactical knowledge.

The queen also established a strict hierarchy within the military, ensuring that positions of authority were filled by capable and loyal individuals. This allowed for efficient command and control during military campaigns and ensured that her orders were carried out effectively. Ranavalona I personally oversaw the training and discipline of her troops, instilling a sense of loyalty and dedication among her soldiers.

Expansionist Policies

QUEEN RANAVALONA I was a visionary leader who sought to expand the borders of her kingdom and increase its influence in the region. She recognized the strategic importance of controlling key trade routes and resources, which would not only enhance the wealth of her kingdom but also strengthen its military capabilities.

Under her rule, Madagascar embarked on a series of military campaigns to conquer neighboring territories. The queen employed a combination of diplomatic negotiations, strategic alliances, and military force to achieve her objectives. She skillfully exploited the rivalries and divisions among neighboring kingdoms, often playing them against each other to weaken their resistance.

Ranavalona I's expansionist policies were not without opposition. Many neighboring kingdoms resisted her advances, leading to fierce battles and prolonged conflicts. However, her military prowess and determination allowed her to overcome these challenges and gradually expand her kingdom's territory.

Fortification and Defensive Strategies

RECOGNIZING THE IMPORTANCE of defending her kingdom against potential invasions, Queen Ranavalona I implemented a series of fortification and defensive strategies. She ordered the construction of fortified cities and strongholds strategically located across Madagascar, providing a line of defense against external threats.

The queen also invested in the development of advanced weaponry and military technology. She encouraged the production of firearms, cannons, and other modern weapons, which gave her forces a significant advantage over her adversaries. These advancements in military technology further solidified her kingdom's defensive capabilities and deterred potential invaders.

Intelligence and Espionage

QUEEN RANAVALONA I understood the importance of gathering intelligence on her enemies and potential threats. She established a network of spies and informants, both within her kingdom and in neighboring territories, to gather valuable information about the intentions and activities of rival kingdoms.

The queen's intelligence network provided her with crucial insights into the military strategies and weaknesses of her adversaries. This allowed her to plan her military campaigns more effectively, exploit vulnerabilities, and achieve decisive victories. The information gathered through espionage also helped her in diplomatic negotiations, giving her an upper hand in dealing with rival kingdoms.

Legacy of Military Policies

QUEEN RANAVALONA I'S consolidation of power and implementation of military policies had a lasting impact on Madagascar. Her strong military ensured the stability and security of her kingdom, deterring potential invaders and maintaining internal order. The expansionist policies she pursued expanded the influence and territory of Madagascar, establishing it as a regional power.

The fortifications and defensive strategies implemented by Ranavalona I continued to protect Madagascar long after her reign. The advancements in military technology and the emphasis on training and discipline laid the foundation for a strong and capable military force that would defend the kingdom for generations to come.

Furthermore, the intelligence and espionage network established by the queen set a precedent for future rulers, highlighting the importance of gathering information and understanding the intentions of rival kingdoms. This legacy of military policies shaped the future of Madagascar and contributed to its resilience in the face of external threats.

Queen Ranavalona I's reign was marked by her unwavering commitment to the defense and expansion of her kingdom. Her consolidation of power and implementation of military policies ensured the stability and security of Madagascar, leaving a lasting legacy that would be remembered for centuries to come.

Persecution of Christians and Legacy

QUEEN RANAVALONA I of Madagascar was a powerful and controversial ruler who reigned from 1828 to 1861. During her time as queen, she implemented a policy of persecution against Christians in Madagascar. This policy, known as the "Persecution of Christians," had a significant impact on the island's religious landscape and left a lasting legacy.

Background and Religious Landscape

BEFORE DELVING INTO the persecution of Christians under Queen Ranavalona I, it is essential to understand the religious landscape of Madagascar during her reign. The majority of the Malagasy people practiced traditional indigenous religions, which were deeply rooted in ancestor worship and animism. However, in the early 19th century, Christian missionaries began arriving on the island, primarily from Europe and the United States.

These missionaries sought to convert the Malagasy people to Christianity, primarily Protestantism. They established schools, churches, and medical facilities, and their influence began to grow steadily. As a result, a significant number of Malagasy people, particularly in coastal areas, converted to Christianity.

Queen Ranavalona I's Policies

QUEEN RANAVALONA I, a staunch defender of traditional Malagasy culture and religion, viewed the spread of Christianity as a threat to her authority and the stability of the kingdom. She believed that the Christian missionaries were undermining the traditional beliefs and customs of the Malagasy people. As a result, she implemented a series of policies aimed at suppressing the growth of Christianity and preserving the indigenous religious practices.

One of the most significant measures taken by Queen Ranavalona I was the prohibition of the practice of Christianity. She issued a royal decree in 1835, which banned the preaching and practice of Christianity throughout the kingdom. This decree was strictly enforced, and those found practicing Christianity were subjected to severe punishment, including imprisonment, torture, and even death.

Methods of Persecution

TO ENFORCE THE BAN on Christianity, Queen Ranavalona I employed various methods of persecution. Christian churches and schools were destroyed, and missionaries were expelled from the island. Malagasy Christians were forced to renounce their faith or face dire consequences. Many Christians went into hiding or practiced their faith secretly to avoid persecution.

The queen also established a network of spies and informants to identify Christians and report their activities to the authorities. This created an atmosphere of fear and suspicion within the kingdom, as people were afraid to openly express their Christian beliefs.

Legacy of Persecution

THE PERSECUTION OF Christians under Queen Ranavalona I had a profound and lasting impact on the religious landscape of Madagascar. While the immediate goal of suppressing Christianity was achieved during her reign, the long-term consequences were more complex.

The persecution led to the martyrdom of many Malagasy Christians who refused to renounce their faith. These individuals became symbols of resistance and inspired future generations to hold onto their Christian beliefs. The stories of their courage and sacrifice were passed down through oral tradition and became an integral part of Malagasy Christian identity.

Furthermore, the persecution of Christians under Queen Ranavalona I contributed to the growth of a unique form of Christianity in Madagascar. The underground nature of the faith during this period fostered a sense of resilience and determination among Malagasy Christians. It also led to the development of indigenous Christian practices that incorporated elements of traditional Malagasy culture and spirituality.

Contemporary Perspectives

THE PERSECUTION OF Christians under Queen Ranavalona I remains a contentious and sensitive topic in Madagascar today. While some view her actions as necessary to protect the indigenous culture and religion of the Malagasy people, others see it as a violation of religious freedom and human rights.

In recent years, there have been efforts to reconcile the legacy of persecution and promote religious tolerance in Madagascar. Interfaith dialogues and initiatives have been established to foster understanding and respect between different religious communities. Additionally, the Malagasy government has taken steps to protect religious freedom and ensure that all citizens can practice their faith without fear of persecution.

Despite the dark chapter of persecution, Queen Ranavalona I's reign also saw significant advancements in other areas. She implemented policies to strengthen the economy, expand trade, and protect Madagascar from European colonization. Her legacy is complex, and it is essential to examine her rule in its entirety, considering both the positive and negative aspects.

In conclusion, the persecution of Christians under Queen Ranavalona I of Madagascar was a significant event in the island's history.

While it aimed to suppress the growth of Christianity, it also had unintended consequences, leading to the development of a resilient and unique form of Malagasy Christianity. Today, efforts are being made to reconcile the legacy of persecution and promote religious tolerance in Madagascar.

Queen Amanirenas of Kush

Kushite Kingdom and Roman Invasion

The Kushite Kingdom, also known as the Kingdom of Kush, was a powerful ancient African civilization that flourished in the region of Nubia, which is present-day Sudan. The kingdom was renowned for its military might, strategic prowess, and the remarkable queens who led their people in times of war. One such remarkable queen was Amanirenas, who played a pivotal role in defending her kingdom against the Roman invasion.

The Rise of the Kushite Kingdom

THE KUSHITE KINGDOM emerged as a powerful force in the ancient world around the 8th century BCE. Situated along the Nile River, the kingdom benefited from its strategic location, which facilitated trade and cultural exchange with neighboring civilizations. Over time, the Kushites developed a sophisticated society, with a strong military and a rich cultural heritage.

Roman Expansion and the Invasion of Kush

DURING THE REIGN OF Emperor Augustus, the Roman Empire sought to expand its territories and influence beyond the Mediterranean. The Romans set their sights on the rich lands of Nubia, which were known for their abundant resources, including gold, ivory, and exotic goods. In 24 BCE, the Roman general, Petronius, led a military campaign to conquer the Kushite Kingdom.

Amanirenas' Resistance and Military Campaigns

AMANIRENAS, THE QUEEN of Kush, was a formidable leader who fiercely resisted the Roman invasion. She rallied her people and led them into battle against the Roman forces. Amanirenas employed various military strategies, including guerrilla warfare and surprise attacks, to weaken the Roman army and disrupt their advance.

Under Amanirenas' leadership, the Kushite warriors displayed great courage and determination. They utilized their knowledge of the terrain and their superior archery skills to inflict heavy casualties on the Roman troops. The queen herself was known for her bravery and tactical brilliance, inspiring her soldiers to fight with unwavering loyalty.

The Battle of Primis and the Roman Retreat

ONE OF THE MOST SIGNIFICANT battles between the Kushites and the Romans was the Battle of Primis. Amanirenas led her forces in a fierce confrontation against the Roman army, which had established a stronghold in the city of Primis. The Kushites launched a relentless assault, overwhelming the Roman defenses and forcing them into retreat.

The Roman invasion of Kush proved to be a costly endeavor for the empire. The Kushite warriors, led by Amanirenas, inflicted heavy losses on the Roman forces, both in terms of soldiers and resources. The Romans realized that conquering Kush would not be an easy task and eventually decided to withdraw their troops from the region.

Peace Treaty and Legacy

FOLLOWING THE ROMAN retreat, Amanirenas negotiated a peace treaty with the Roman Empire. The terms of the treaty ensured the independence of the Kushite Kingdom and secured its borders from further Roman aggression. Amanirenas' successful defense of her kingdom against a formidable empire solidified her reputation as a warrior queen and a symbol of resistance.

The legacy of Amanirenas and the Kushite Kingdom extends beyond their military achievements. The Kushites were known for their advanced civilization, with impressive architectural feats such as the pyramids of Meroe. They also had a rich cultural heritage, blending elements of Egyptian, Nubian, and African traditions.

Amanirenas' resistance against the Roman invasion serves as a testament to the strength and resilience of the Kushite people. Her leadership and military prowess continue to inspire generations, highlighting the significant role that warrior queens played in shaping African history.

In conclusion, the Kushite Kingdom, under the leadership of Queen Amanirenas, faced the Roman invasion with determination and courage. Through her strategic military campaigns and the Battle of Primis, Amanirenas successfully defended her kingdom and secured its independence. Her legacy as a warrior queen and symbol of resistance remains an integral part of African history, showcasing the strength and power of female leaders in ancient civilizations.

Amanirenas' Resistance and Military Campaigns

QUEEN AMANIRENAS OF Kush was a formidable warrior queen who led her kingdom in a fierce resistance against the Roman Empire. Her military campaigns and strategic brilliance made her a legendary figure in African history. Amanirenas' determination and courage inspired her people to fight for their freedom and independence, leaving a lasting legacy that continues to resonate today.

The Roman Invasion

DURING THE REIGN OF Amanirenas, the Kushite Kingdom faced a significant threat from the Roman Empire. In 24 BCE, the Roman Emperor Augustus sent his general, Petronius, to conquer the wealthy and powerful kingdom of Kush. The Romans saw Kush as a valuable territory due to its abundant resources, including gold and other precious commodities.

Amanirenas' Resistance

AMANIRENAS REFUSED to submit to Roman rule and rallied her people to resist the invasion. She led her army into battle, displaying exceptional military prowess and strategic acumen. Amanirenas understood the importance of guerrilla warfare and utilized her knowledge of the terrain to her advantage. Her forces launched surprise attacks on the Roman legions, inflicting heavy casualties and disrupting their supply lines.

Military Campaigns

UNDER AMANIRENAS' LEADERSHIP, the Kushite army launched a series of military campaigns against the Roman forces. They engaged in fierce battles, employing various tactics to weaken and demoralize the enemy. Amanirenas' forces utilized their superior knowledge of the terrain, ambushing the Romans and utilizing hit-and-run tactics to wear them down.

One of the most significant military campaigns led by Amanirenas was the Battle of Primis. In this battle, the Kushite forces launched a surprise attack on the Roman garrison at Primis, a strategic stronghold. Amanirenas' army overwhelmed the Romans, forcing them to retreat and securing a crucial victory for the Kushite Kingdom.

Siege of Aswan

AMANIRENAS' MOST FAMOUS military campaign was the siege of Aswan, a Roman-controlled city located on the Nile River. Determined to liberate her people from Roman oppression, Amanirenas led a relentless assault on the city. Her forces laid siege to Aswan, cutting off its supply lines and isolating the Roman garrison.

The siege of Aswan lasted for several months, during which Amanirenas' army launched numerous attacks on the city's defenses. The Kushite warriors displayed incredible bravery and resilience, enduring harsh conditions and fierce Roman resistance. Despite facing a well-equipped and disciplined Roman army, Amanirenas' forces never wavered in their determination to reclaim their land.

Peace Treaty and Legacy

AMANIRENAS' MILITARY campaigns eventually forced the Romans to negotiate a peace treaty. The Romans recognized the strength and resilience of the Kushite Kingdom and agreed to withdraw their forces from Kushite territory. This peace treaty secured the independence of the Kushite Kingdom and solidified Amanirenas' legacy as a warrior queen who successfully defended her people against a powerful empire.

Amanirenas' resistance and military campaigns left an indelible mark on African history. Her bravery and leadership continue to inspire generations of Africans, particularly women, to stand up against oppression and fight for their rights. Amanirenas' legacy serves as a reminder of the strength and resilience of African women throughout history.

Peace Treaty and Legacy

AFTER YEARS OF FIERCE resistance and military campaigns against the Roman Empire, Queen Amanirenas of Kush eventually sought a peaceful resolution to the conflict. Recognizing the toll that war had taken on her people and the need for stability, she engaged in diplomatic negotiations with the Roman Emperor Augustus. This resulted in the signing of a peace treaty that brought an end to the hostilities between the Kushite Kingdom and the Roman Empire.

Negotiations and Terms of the Peace Treaty

THE NEGOTIATIONS BETWEEN Queen Amanirenas and Emperor Augustus were conducted with the aim of establishing a lasting peace between the two powers. Both leaders recognized the futility of continued warfare and the potential benefits of cooperation. The terms of the peace treaty were carefully negotiated to ensure the interests of both parties were addressed.

Under the terms of the treaty, the Roman Empire agreed to withdraw its forces from Kushite territory and cease any further military campaigns against the kingdom. In return, Queen Amanirenas agreed to recognize Roman authority and maintain peaceful relations with the empire. The treaty also included provisions for trade and cultural exchange between the two powers, fostering a sense of mutual understanding and cooperation.

Impact and Legacy of the Peace Treaty

THE PEACE TREATY BETWEEN Queen Amanirenas and Emperor Augustus had a profound impact on the Kushite Kingdom and its relationship with the Roman Empire. It marked a significant turning point in the history of the region, shifting the focus from conflict to diplomacy and cooperation.

The treaty allowed the Kushite Kingdom to rebuild and recover from the devastating effects of the Roman invasion. With the cessation of hostilities, the kingdom could redirect its resources towards development, infrastructure, and the well-being of its people. Trade flourished between Kush and the Roman Empire, bringing economic prosperity to both regions.

The legacy of the peace treaty extended beyond the immediate benefits of peace and economic growth. It set a precedent for diplomatic negotiations and peaceful resolutions to conflicts, demonstrating the power of dialogue and compromise. Queen Amanirenas' willingness to engage in diplomacy showcased her strategic thinking and her commitment to the well-being of her people.

Queen Amanirenas' Enduring Legacy

QUEEN AMANIRENAS' LEGACY extends far beyond the peace treaty she negotiated with the Roman Empire. Her unwavering determination, military prowess, and diplomatic skills continue to inspire generations of Africans and women around the world.

Her resistance against the Roman Empire serves as a testament to the indomitable spirit of the Kushite people and their refusal to be subjugated. Amanirenas' military campaigns and strategic victories against a formidable enemy highlight her exceptional leadership and tactical brilliance.

Furthermore, her decision to seek a peaceful resolution through diplomacy demonstrates her wisdom and foresight. By prioritizing the well-being of her people and recognizing the benefits of cooperation, she set an example for leaders to follow.

Queen Amanirenas' legacy also serves as a reminder of the significant role that women played in African history. As a warrior queen, she defied societal norms and shattered gender stereotypes, proving that women were just as capable of leading armies and shaping the course of history.

Her story continues to inspire women to embrace their strength, resilience, and leadership potential. Queen Amanirenas' legacy serves as a powerful symbol of female empowerment and the importance of recognizing and celebrating the contributions of women in history.

In conclusion, the peace treaty negotiated by Queen Amanirenas with the Roman Empire marked a pivotal moment in the history of the Kushite Kingdom. It brought an end to years of conflict and paved the way for peaceful relations and mutual cooperation. Queen Amanirenas' legacy as a warrior queen and diplomat continues to inspire and empower people, reminding us of the enduring impact of female warriors in African history.

Queen Nandi of the Zulu Kingdom

Early Life and Motherhood

Queen Nandi of the Zulu Kingdom was not only a formidable warrior but also a remarkable mother. Her early life and experiences shaped her into the influential figure she would become, leaving a lasting impact on Zulu culture and warfare.

Childhood and Upbringing

NANDI WAS BORN IN THE early 1760s in the Langeni clan, a small community within the larger Zulu tribe. Her father, Bhebhe, was the chief of the Langeni, and her mother, Mbhengi, was a Sangoma, a traditional healer and spiritual guide. Nandi's upbringing was deeply rooted in Zulu traditions and customs, and she was taught the importance of honor, bravery, and loyalty from a young age.

Challenges and Exile

NANDI'S EARLY LIFE was marked by adversity. Her father's enemies within the tribe sought to undermine his authority, leading to his exile. As a result, Nandi and her mother were also forced to leave their home and seek refuge in neighboring communities. This period of exile was a challenging time for Nandi, but it also served as a catalyst for her resilience and determination.

During her exile, Nandi faced discrimination and mistreatment from those who saw her as an outcast. However, she refused to let these hardships define her. Instead, she drew strength from her mother's teachings and the support of her community, vowing to overcome the obstacles in her path.

Motherhood and Shaka Zulu

NANDI'S MOST SIGNIFICANT role in life was that of a mother. She gave birth to a son named Shaka, who would later become one of the most renowned leaders in African history. Nandi's love and devotion to her son were unwavering, and she played a crucial role in shaping his character and preparing him for the challenges he would face as a future king.

As a single mother, Nandi faced numerous hardships while raising Shaka. She instilled in him a sense of pride in his Zulu heritage and taught him the importance of courage and discipline. Nandi's influence on Shaka was profound, and he often sought her counsel and guidance throughout his life.

Nandi's Impact on Zulu Warfare

NANDI'S EXPERIENCES and teachings had a profound impact on Zulu warfare. She understood the importance of discipline, strategy, and unity in battle, and she passed these principles onto her son. Nandi's influence on Shaka's military tactics and organization was instrumental in the success of the Zulu Kingdom.

Under Shaka's rule, the Zulu army became a formidable force, known for its innovative battle formations and fierce warriors. Nandi's emphasis on discipline and unity laid the foundation for the Zulu's military prowess, enabling them to conquer neighboring tribes and establish a powerful empire.

Nandi's Legacy and Cultural Significance

NANDI'S LEGACY EXTENDS far beyond her role as a mother and advisor to Shaka. She is revered as a symbol of strength, resilience, and maternal love in Zulu culture. Her story serves as an inspiration to women and men alike, highlighting the significant contributions that women can make in shaping history.

Nandi's influence on Zulu culture can still be seen today. Her teachings on discipline and unity continue to resonate within the Zulu community, and her legacy as a warrior queen has become an integral part of Zulu folklore and traditions. Nandi's story reminds us of the power of a mother's love and the lasting impact that one individual can have on an entire nation.

In conclusion, Nandi's early life and motherhood played a crucial role in shaping her into the influential figure she became. Her experiences of exile, challenges, and resilience molded her into a strong and determined leader. As a mother, Nandi's love and guidance had a profound impact on her son, Shaka, and the Zulu Kingdom as a whole. Her legacy as a warrior queen and symbol of strength continues to inspire and empower generations of Zulu people.

Influence on Shaka Zulu and Zulu Warfare

QUEEN NANDI OF THE Zulu Kingdom played a significant role in shaping the future of the Zulu nation and had a profound influence on her son, Shaka Zulu, who would go on to become one of Africa's most renowned military leaders. Nandi's strength, resilience, and unwavering support for her son laid the foundation for the Zulu Kingdom's military prowess and the development of innovative warfare strategies.

Nandi's Impact on Shaka Zulu's Upbringing

NANDI, BORN INTO THE Langeni clan, faced numerous challenges throughout her life. Despite being an outcast due to her illegitimate birth, she possessed a fierce determination and an indomitable spirit. Nandi's strength and resilience were instilled in her son, Shaka, from a young age. She taught him the importance of perseverance, courage, and self-belief, which would later shape his leadership style and military strategies.

Nandi's influence on Shaka's upbringing was profound. She nurtured his natural talents and encouraged him to embrace his warrior spirit. She taught him the art of warfare, instilling in him a deep understanding of Zulu traditions, customs, and the importance of unity within the tribe. Nandi's unwavering support and belief in her son's abilities played a crucial role in shaping his character and preparing him for the challenges that lay ahead.

Shaka Zulu's Military Reforms

UNDER SHAKA'S LEADERSHIP, the Zulu Kingdom underwent a significant transformation in terms of military organization and tactics. Shaka revolutionized Zulu warfare by introducing innovative strategies and implementing military reforms that would make the Zulu army a formidable force.

One of the most significant reforms introduced by Shaka was the creation of the impi, a highly disciplined and well-trained fighting force. Shaka reorganized the Zulu warriors into regiments, each with its own distinctive shield and spear. He emphasized the importance of physical fitness, discipline, and loyalty within the ranks of the impi. Shaka's military reforms focused on creating a cohesive and efficient army that could swiftly adapt to changing battlefield conditions.

The Assegai and the Bull Horn Formation

SHAKA ZULU'S MILITARY innovations extended to the weaponry and tactics employed by the Zulu warriors. He introduced the short stabbing spear known as the assegai, which became the primary weapon of the Zulu army. The assegai was lightweight, versatile, and deadly in close combat, giving the Zulu warriors a significant advantage on the battlefield.

Shaka also developed a tactical formation known as the Bull Horn formation. This formation involved dividing the Zulu army into three sections: the "chest," the "horns," and the "loins." The chest formed the main body of the army, while the horns and loins flanked the enemy, encircling them and creating a deadly trap. This formation allowed the Zulu warriors to surround and overwhelm their opponents, leading to numerous victories on the battlefield.

Shaka's Legacy and the Zulu Empire

SHAKA ZULU'S MILITARY successes and his establishment of the Zulu Empire can be attributed, in part, to the influence of his mother, Queen Nandi. Nandi's teachings and guidance shaped Shaka's leadership style and military strategies, enabling him to create a powerful and highly organized army.

Under Shaka's rule, the Zulu Empire expanded its territory through a series of military campaigns and conquests. The Zulu warriors, trained in Shaka's innovative tactics, became renowned for their discipline, bravery, and ferocity in battle. The Zulu Empire reached its zenith under Shaka's leadership, becoming a dominant force in southern Africa.

The Enduring Legacy of Nandi and Shaka Zulu

NANDI'S INFLUENCE ON Shaka Zulu and the Zulu Kingdom cannot be overstated. Her strength, resilience, and unwavering support laid the foundation for the Zulu Empire's military prowess and the development of innovative warfare strategies. Shaka's military reforms and tactics revolutionized Zulu warfare and left a lasting impact on the history of African military strategies.

The legacy of Nandi and Shaka Zulu continues to inspire and captivate people around the world. Their story serves as a testament to the indomitable spirit of African warrior queens and the significant role they played in shaping the history of the continent. The Zulu Kingdom's military achievements under Shaka's leadership stand as a testament to the enduring legacy of Nandi and her influence on her son. Their story serves as a reminder of the strength, resilience, and leadership of African women throughout history.

Legacy and Cultural Significance

THE LEGACY AND CULTURAL significance of Queen Nandi of the Zulu Kingdom are profound and far-reaching. As the mother of Shaka Zulu, she played a pivotal role in shaping the Zulu nation and its military prowess. Her influence on Zulu warfare and her unwavering support for her son left an indelible mark on the history and culture of the Zulu people.

Nandi's Influence on Zulu Society

QUEEN NANDI'S IMPACT on Zulu society cannot be overstated. Her strength, resilience, and determination served as an inspiration for generations to come. Nandi's unwavering belief in the power of her people and her commitment to their well-being laid the foundation for the Zulu Kingdom's rise to prominence.

The Power of Motherhood

NANDI'S ROLE AS A MOTHER was instrumental in shaping the destiny of the Zulu Kingdom. She instilled in her son, Shaka, a sense of pride, discipline, and loyalty to his people. Nandi's love and guidance provided Shaka with the emotional support he needed to become the formidable warrior and leader he would later become.

Nandi's Influence on Zulu Warfare

QUEEN NANDI'S INFLUENCE on Zulu warfare cannot be underestimated. She introduced innovative military strategies and tactics that revolutionized the Zulu army. Nandi's emphasis on discipline, agility, and bravery transformed the Zulu warriors into a formidable force that struck fear into the hearts of their enemies.

The Cultural Significance of Queen Nandi

QUEEN NANDI'S LEGACY extends beyond her military contributions. She is revered as a symbol of strength, resilience, and maternal love within Zulu culture. Her story serves as a reminder of the power of women and the vital role they play in shaping societies.

Nandi's Influence on Gender Roles

NANDI'S INFLUENCE CHALLENGED traditional gender roles within Zulu society. Her strength and leadership qualities shattered the notion that women were solely confined to domestic duties. Nandi's example empowered women to assert themselves and take on roles traditionally reserved for men.

Nandi's Impact on Zulu Identity

QUEEN NANDI'S IMPACT on Zulu identity is deeply rooted in the cultural fabric of the Zulu people. Her legacy serves as a source of pride and inspiration for Zulu men and women alike. Nandi's story reinforces the idea that strength, courage, and leadership are not limited by gender but are qualities that can be embodied by anyone.

Nandi's Enduring Legacy

QUEEN NANDI'S LEGACY continues to resonate in modern-day South Africa. Her story has been passed down through generations, ensuring that her contributions are not forgotten. Nandi's influence on Zulu society serves as a reminder of the strength and resilience of African women throughout history.

Nandi's Influence on Female Empowerment

QUEEN NANDI'S LIFE and achievements have become a symbol of female empowerment. Her story inspires women to embrace their strength, challenge societal norms, and strive for greatness. Nandi's legacy encourages women to break barriers and pursue their dreams, knowing that they too can leave a lasting impact on their communities and the world.

Nandi's Cultural Significance Today

IN CONTEMPORARY ZULU culture, Queen Nandi is celebrated and honored. Her story is often told through oral traditions, songs, and dances, keeping her memory alive. Nandi's cultural significance serves as a reminder of the rich history and heritage of the Zulu people and their enduring spirit.

Nandi's Influence on African History

QUEEN NANDI'S INFLUENCE extends beyond the borders of the Zulu Kingdom. Her story is a testament to the strength and resilience of African women throughout history. Nandi's legacy stands as a powerful example of the significant contributions that women have made to the development and progress of African societies.

In conclusion, Queen Nandi's legacy and cultural significance are immeasurable. Her influence on Zulu society, warfare, and gender roles have left an indelible mark on the history and culture of the Zulu people. Her story continues to inspire and empower women, serving as a reminder of the strength and resilience of African women throughout history. Queen Nandi's enduring legacy is a testament to the significant contributions that women have made to African history and the ongoing fight for female empowerment.

Queen Kahina of the Berber Kingdom

Berber Resistance against Arab Conquest

The Berber people, also known as Amazigh, have a rich history of resistance against foreign invasions and conquests. One notable period of resistance was during the Arab conquest of North Africa in the 7th century. At the forefront of this resistance was the legendary Queen Kahina, who led her people in a fierce struggle against the Arab forces.

The Arab Conquest of North Africa

IN THE 7TH CENTURY, the Arab armies, driven by the expansion of Islam, began their conquest of North Africa. The Berber people, who had inhabited the region for centuries, fiercely resisted the Arab invaders. The Berbers, known for their strong sense of independence and warrior culture, were determined to defend their lands and way of life.

Queen Kahina's Leadership

QUEEN KAHINA, ALSO known as Dihya, emerged as a prominent leader during this tumultuous period. She was a Berber queen from the Aures Mountains in present-day Algeria. Kahina was known for her exceptional leadership skills, strategic brilliance, and unwavering commitment to the defense of her people.

Military Strategies and Tactics

QUEEN KAHINA EMPLOYED various military strategies and tactics to resist the Arab conquest. She organized and trained her forces, utilizing the rugged terrain of the Atlas Mountains to her advantage. Kahina's army consisted of both men and women, as the Berber society recognized the equal capabilities and contributions of both genders in warfare.

Kahina's forces employed guerrilla warfare tactics, launching surprise attacks on the Arab armies and then retreating to the safety of the mountains. This strategy allowed them to inflict significant damage on the Arab forces while minimizing their own casualties. The Berber warriors, under Kahina's leadership, displayed remarkable resilience and determination in the face of a formidable enemy.

Symbol of Resistance

QUEEN KAHINA BECAME a symbol of resistance against the Arab conquest, inspiring her people to fight for their freedom and cultural identity. Her leadership and bravery instilled a sense of unity among the Berber tribes, who rallied behind her in their struggle against the Arab invaders.

The Battle of Tabarka

ONE OF THE MOST SIGNIFICANT battles of the Berber resistance was the Battle of Tabarka. In this decisive confrontation, Queen Kahina led her forces against the Arab army, inflicting heavy casualties and forcing them to retreat. The Berber victory at Tabarka demonstrated the strength and determination of the resistance movement and dealt a significant blow to the Arab conquest.

Arab-Berber Peace Treaty

DESPITE THE FIERCE resistance, the Arab forces eventually gained the upper hand in the conquest of North Africa. Recognizing the strength and resilience of the Berber resistance, the Arab conquerors sought a peaceful resolution. A peace treaty was negotiated between Queen Kahina and the Arab general Hassan ibn al-Nu'man.

Under the terms of the treaty, the Berbers were allowed to retain their lands and practice their own religion, provided they paid tribute to the Arab rulers. While the peace treaty marked the end of the armed resistance, it also ensured the survival of the Berber culture and identity in the face of Arab domination.

Legacy and Cultural Significance

QUEEN KAHINA'S LEGACY as a fearless warrior and symbol of resistance against foreign domination continues to inspire the Berber people to this day. Her leadership and military strategies have become an integral part of Berber folklore and history. Kahina's resistance against the Arab conquest serves as a reminder of the indomitable spirit and determination of the Berber people in preserving their cultural heritage.

The Berber resistance against the Arab conquest also highlights the significant role played by women in warfare and leadership. Queen Kahina shattered gender stereotypes and proved that women were just as capable as men in defending their people and lands. Her legacy serves as a testament to the strength and resilience of female warriors throughout African history.

In conclusion, Queen Kahina's leadership and the Berber resistance against the Arab conquest of North Africa stand as a testament to the courage and determination of the Berber people. Their struggle for independence and cultural preservation serves as an inspiration for future generations, highlighting the importance of preserving one's identity and heritage in the face of foreign domination. Queen Kahina's legacy as a warrior queen and symbol of resistance continues to resonate in the hearts of the Berber people, reminding them of their rich history and the strength of their ancestors.

Kahina's Leadership and Military Strategies

QUEEN KAHINA, ALSO known as Dihya, was a remarkable leader and military strategist who played a crucial role in the resistance against the Arab conquest of the Berber Kingdom in North Africa. Her leadership and military strategies were instrumental in defending her people and preserving their culture and way of life.

Early Life and Rise to Power

KAHINA WAS BORN INTO a noble Berber family in the region of Numidia, which is present-day Algeria. She grew up in a society that valued courage, independence, and the preservation of their ancestral traditions. From a young age, Kahina displayed exceptional intelligence, bravery, and a deep understanding of her people's history and culture.

As she matured, Kahina became increasingly aware of the growing threat posed by the Arab invaders who sought to conquer and convert the Berber people. Recognizing the need for strong leadership, Kahina emerged as a prominent figure within her community, rallying her people to resist the Arab conquest.

Military Strategies and Tactics

KAHINA'S MILITARY STRATEGIES were characterized by a combination of guerrilla warfare, defensive tactics, and diplomatic maneuvering. She understood the importance of adapting to the changing circumstances of war and utilized her knowledge of the local terrain to her advantage.

One of Kahina's key military strategies was the use of hit-and-run tactics. Her forces would launch surprise attacks on Arab encampments, inflicting heavy casualties before retreating into the mountains and deserts where they held the advantage. This strategy allowed her forces to weaken the Arab invaders while minimizing their own losses.

Kahina also employed defensive tactics to protect her people and their territories. She ordered the construction of fortified positions and utilized natural barriers such as mountains and rivers to create defensive lines. These fortifications served as strongholds from which her forces could launch counterattacks and repel Arab advances.

In addition to her military prowess, Kahina was a skilled diplomat. She recognized the importance of forging alliances with neighboring tribes and kingdoms who shared a common interest in resisting Arab domination. Through her diplomatic efforts, Kahina was able to form a coalition of Berber tribes, uniting them under a common cause and strengthening their resistance against the Arab invaders.

Leadership and Inspiration

KAHINA'S LEADERSHIP style was characterized by her unwavering determination, charisma, and ability to inspire her people. She led by example, fearlessly leading her troops into battle and demonstrating her commitment to the cause. Her courage and resilience in the face of adversity inspired her followers to fight with unwavering loyalty and dedication.

As a leader, Kahina was known for her strategic thinking and ability to make difficult decisions. She understood the importance of balancing short-term gains with long-term objectives, often making sacrifices for the greater good of her people. Her ability to inspire trust and loyalty among her followers was a testament to her leadership skills.

Legacy and Symbolism

QUEEN KAHINA'S LEGACY extends far beyond her military achievements. She became a symbol of resistance and a source of inspiration for future generations. Her unwavering determination and refusal to surre

Her legacy serves as a reminder of the strength and resilience of the Berber people and their nder in the face of overwhelming odds continue to inspire individuals who strive for freedom and independence.

Kahina's leadership and military strategies left a lasting impact on the Berber people. Her resistance against the Arab conquest delayed their advance and preserved the Berber culture and way of life.enduring spirit.

Today, Queen Kahina is celebrated as a national hero in Algeria and a symbol of Berber resistance. Her story serves as a testament to the power of leadership, courage, and determination in the face of adversity. Queen Kahina's contributions to the history of Africa and her role as a warrior queen continue to inspire and empower individuals around the world.

Legacy and Symbolism

THE LEGACY OF QUEEN Kahina of the Berber Kingdom is one that continues to inspire and symbolize the strength and resilience of African women throughout history. Her impact on the Berber resistance against Arab conquest and her leadership in the face of adversity have left an indelible mark on African history and culture. The symbolism associated with Queen Kahina resonates with the struggles and triumphs of women in Africa, serving as a reminder of their power and agency.

Symbol of Resistance

QUEEN KAHINA'S LEGACY is deeply rooted in her unwavering resistance against the Arab conquest of North Africa. She became a symbol of defiance and resilience, leading her people in a fierce battle against the Arab invaders. Her determination to protect her kingdom and preserve the Berber way of life made her an icon of resistance. The story of Queen Kahina serves as a testament to the strength and courage of African women who have fought against colonization and oppression throughout history.

Defender of Culture and Identity

QUEEN KAHINA'S LEADERSHIP was not only characterized by her military strategies but also by her commitment to preserving the cultural identity of her people. She recognized the importance of maintaining the traditions, customs, and beliefs of the Berber Kingdom in the face of Arab influence. Queen Kahina's efforts to protect and promote Berber culture have made her a symbol of cultural preservation and identity. Her legacy serves as a reminder of the significance of cultural heritage and the importance of safeguarding it for future generations.

Empowerment and Equality

QUEEN KAHINA'S REIGN challenged traditional gender roles and norms of her time. As a female leader in a predominantly patriarchal society, she defied societal expectations and proved that women were capable of leading and defending their communities. Queen Kahina's empowerment of women and her belief in their abilities have made her an emblem of gender equality and women's empowerment. Her legacy continues to inspire women across Africa to break barriers and strive for equality in all aspects of life.

Inspiration for Leadership

QUEEN KAHINA'S LEADERSHIP qualities and strategic military tactics have made her an enduring source of inspiration for leaders in Africa and beyond. Her ability to unite her people, strategize against a powerful enemy, and inspire loyalty among her followers serves as a model for effective leadership. Queen Kahina's legacy encourages leaders to be courageous, visionary, and compassionate, and to prioritize the well-being and interests of their communities.

Cultural and Historical Significance

THE STORY OF QUEEN Kahina holds immense cultural and historical significance for the Berber people and the wider African continent. Her resistance against Arab conquest and her efforts to preserve Berber culture have become an integral part of the collective memory and identity of the Berber community. Queen Kahina's legacy serves as a reminder of the rich and diverse history of Africa and the contributions of its female leaders. Her story contributes to a more comprehensive understanding of African history and challenges the dominant narratives that often overlook the achievements of women.

Legacy in Art and Literature

QUEEN KAHINA'S LEGACY has been immortalized in various forms of art and literature. Her story has been depicted in paintings, sculptures, and other artistic mediums, capturing her strength and determination. Additionally, her life and achievements have been celebrated in literature, with numerous books and poems dedicated to her legacy. These artistic representations and literary works not only preserve her memory but also serve as a source of inspiration for future generations.

Continuing the Legacy

THE LEGACY OF QUEEN Kahina serves as a call to action for the empowerment and advancement of women in Africa. It reminds us of the importance of recognizing and celebrating the contributions of women in history and in contemporary society. To continue her legacy, it is crucial to provide equal opportunities for women in education, politics, and leadership roles. By amplifying the voices and stories of

African women, we can ensure that their contributions are acknowledged and their legacies are carried forward.

In conclusion, Queen Kahina's legacy as a symbol of resistance, defender of culture and identity, and advocate for empowerment and equality continues to inspire and resonate with women in Africa. Her story serves as a reminder of the strength, resilience, and leadership capabilities of African women throughout history. By recognizing and celebrating the legacy of Queen Kahina, we can honor the contributions of all warrior queens and pave the way for a more inclusive and equitable future.

Conclusion

Impact of Warrior Queens in African History

Throughout African history, warrior queens have played a significant role in shaping the continent's destiny. These remarkable women defied societal norms and emerged as powerful leaders, warriors, and strategists. Their impact on African history cannot be overstated, as they not only defended their kingdoms but also inspired future generations of women to rise above societal expectations and fight for their rights. The legacy of these warrior queens continues to resonate in African culture, politics, and the ongoing struggle for gender equality.

Challenging Gender Roles

ONE OF THE MOST SIGNIFICANT impacts of warrior queens in African history was their ability to challenge traditional gender roles. In a patriarchal society, where women were often confined to domestic duties, these queens shattered stereotypes and proved that women were just as capable as men in matters of leadership and warfare. By leading armies, making strategic decisions, and engaging in military campaigns, they demonstrated that gender should not be a barrier to achieving greatness.

The presence of warrior queens in African history challenged the notion that women were weak and incapable of participating in the defense of their kingdoms. Their bravery and skill on the battlefield inspired both men and women to question societal norms and recognize the potential of women in positions of power. The impact of these warrior queens extended far beyond their own reigns, as their stories became a source of inspiration for future generations.

Preservation of African Culture

WARRIOR QUEENS PLAYED a crucial role in preserving African culture and traditions. As defenders of their kingdoms, they fought against foreign invaders who sought to impose their own customs and beliefs. These queens understood the importance of protecting their cultural heritage and worked tirelessly to ensure that African traditions were upheld.

By resisting colonization and foreign influence, warrior queens safeguarded African languages, customs, and spiritual practices. They became symbols of resistance and pride, inspiring their people to remain steadfast in the face of adversity. The impact of their efforts can still be seen today, as African culture continues to thrive despite centuries of external pressures.

Empowerment of Women

PERHAPS THE MOST SIGNIFICANT impact of warrior queens in African history was their role in empowering women. By defying societal expectations and excelling in traditionally male-dominated fields, these queens became beacons of hope for women across the continent. Their achievements shattered the notion that women were inferior and incapable of leadership.

The stories of warrior queens served as a source of inspiration for women who aspired to break free from the constraints of gender norms. These queens proved that women could be strong, intelligent, and capable of leading armies. Their impact on the empowerment of women cannot be overstated, as they paved the way for future generations of African women to pursue their dreams and challenge societal limitations.

Influence on Political Landscape

WARRIOR QUEENS ALSO had a profound impact on the political landscape of Africa. Through their leadership and military prowess, they not only defended their kingdoms but also expanded their territories and influence. Their strategic decisions and diplomatic skills allowed them to navigate complex political situations and forge alliances with neighboring kingdoms.

The influence of warrior queens extended beyond their own realms, as their actions often had far-reaching consequences. Their military campaigns and diplomatic efforts shaped the balance of power in Africa, leaving a lasting impact on the political landscape of the continent. Their ability to unite disparate groups and defend their kingdoms against external threats demonstrated their exceptional leadership skills and political acumen.

Inspiration for Future Generations

THE IMPACT OF WARRIOR queens in African history continues to inspire future generations. Their stories serve as a reminder of the strength, resilience, and determination of African women. The legacy of these queens lives on in the hearts and minds of those who seek to challenge societal norms and fight for equality.

The lessons learned from the lives of warrior queens are invaluable. They teach us the importance of courage, perseverance, and the pursuit of justice. Their stories remind us that greatness knows no gender and that anyone, regardless of societal expectations, can rise to positions of power and influence.

Conclusion

THE IMPACT OF WARRIOR queens in African history cannot be overstated. These remarkable women challenged gender roles, preserved African culture, empowered women, influenced the political landscape, and continue to inspire future generations. Their contributions have left an indelible mark on African history and serve as a testament to the strength and resilience of African women. As we continue to strive for gender equality and empowerment, the legacy of these warrior queens will forever be a source of inspiration and guidance.

Lessons from the Lives of Warrior Queens

THE LIVES OF WARRIOR queens from ancient African civilizations provide us with valuable lessons that can be applied to various aspects of life. These remarkable women defied societal norms, challenged oppressive forces, and left a lasting impact on history. Their stories offer inspiration and guidance for individuals seeking empowerment, leadership, and resilience. Here are some key lessons we can learn from the lives of warrior queens:

Embracing Courage and Determination

ONE OF THE MOST PROMINENT lessons we can learn from warrior queens is the importance of embracing courage and determination. These women faced numerous challenges and obstacles, yet they never backed down. They displayed unwavering bravery in the face of adversity, whether it was battling foreign invaders, leading armies, or defending their kingdoms. Their stories teach us the significance of standing up for what we believe in, even when the odds are against us.

Breaking Gender Stereotypes

THE LIVES OF WARRIOR queens shattered gender stereotypes and challenged societal expectations. They proved that women are just as capable as men in leadership roles and on the battlefield. By defying traditional gender roles, these queens paved the way for future generations of women to pursue their dreams and aspirations. Their stories remind us that gender should never be a barrier to achieving greatness.

Strategic Thinking and Military Tactics

WARRIOR QUEENS WERE not only fierce warriors but also skilled strategists. They possessed a deep understanding of military tactics and employed innovative strategies to outwit their enemies. From Queen Nzinga's diplomatic negotiations to Queen Amina's military campaigns, these women showcased the power of strategic thinking. Their stories teach us the importance of planning, adaptability, and critical thinking in overcoming challenges.

Resilience in the Face of Adversity

THE LIVES OF WARRIOR queens are a testament to the power of resilience. They faced numerous setbacks, including colonization, invasions, and internal conflicts. However, they never gave up. Instead, they rose from the ashes, rebuilt their kingdoms, and continued to fight for their people. Their stories inspire us to persevere in the face of adversity, to never lose hope, and to find strength in our darkest moments.

Empowering Others and Building Alliances

WARRIOR QUEENS UNDERSTOOD the importance of empowering others and building alliances. They recognized that unity and collaboration were essential for success. Queen Yaa Asantewaa, for example, rallied her people and led a resistance against British colonialism. These queens taught us the significance of lifting others up, fostering a sense of community, and working together towards a common goal.

Preserving Cultural Heritage

THE WARRIOR QUEENS of Africa were not only military leaders but also custodians of their cultural heritage. They took pride in their traditions, languages, and customs, and fought to preserve them. Queen Makeda's legacy, for instance, is deeply intertwined with the cultural impact she had on Ethiopia. These queens remind us of the importance of preserving our cultural heritage and passing it on to future generations.

Inspiring Female Empowerment

PERHAPS THE MOST SIGNIFICANT lesson we can learn from warrior queens is the importance of female empowerment. These women defied societal norms and paved the way for future generations of women to rise to positions of power and influence. Their stories inspire us to challenge gender inequality, advocate for women's rights, and create a more inclusive society. They remind us that women have always played a vital role in shaping history and deserve equal opportunities.

Leading with Compassion and Justice

WARRIOR QUEENS WERE not only fierce warriors but also compassionate leaders. They governed with a sense of justice, fairness, and empathy. Queen Amanirenas, for example, negotiated a peace treaty with the Roman Empire to protect her people. These queens teach us the importance of leading with compassion, treating others with respect, and striving for justice in all aspects of life.

Embracing Cultural Diversity

THE WARRIOR QUEENS of Africa embraced cultural diversity and recognized the strength that comes from unity. They formed alliances with neighboring kingdoms, embraced different languages and traditions, and celebrated diversity. Their stories remind us of the richness that comes from embracing different cultures and the importance of fostering inclusivity in our communities.

Leaving a Lasting Legacy

FINALLY, THE LIVES of warrior queens teach us the significance of leaving a lasting legacy. These women's actions and achievements continue to inspire and influence generations long after their time. Their stories remind us of the impact we can have on the world and the importance of leaving a positive mark on history.

In conclusion, the lives of warrior queens from ancient African civilizations provide us with invaluable lessons. From embracing courage and breaking gender stereotypes to strategic thinking and resilience, these women's stories inspire us to be better leaders, advocates, and individuals. By learning from their experiences, we can continue their legacy of female empowerment, cultural preservation, and justice for generations to come.

Continuing the Legacy of Female Empowerment

THROUGHOUT HISTORY, warrior queens have played a significant role in shaping the world we live in today. These remarkable women defied societal norms and expectations, leading armies, defending their kingdoms, and leaving a lasting impact on African history. Their stories continue to inspire and empower women around the world. In this final chapter, we will explore how we can continue the legacy of female empowerment that these warrior queens have left behind.

Education and Empowerment

ONE OF THE MOST CRUCIAL ways to continue the legacy of female empowerment is through education. By providing girls and women with access to quality education, we can equip them with the knowledge and skills necessary to pursue their dreams and aspirations.

Education not only empowers women to become leaders in their communities but also enables them to challenge societal norms and break through barriers.

It is essential to promote gender equality in education by ensuring equal opportunities for girls and boys. By eliminating gender disparities in education, we can create a more inclusive society where women have the same chances to succeed as men. This can be achieved through policies that prioritize girls' education, provide scholarships and financial support, and encourage girls to pursue traditionally male-dominated fields such as science, technology, engineering, and mathematics (STEM).

Leadership and Representation

ANOTHER WAY TO CONTINUE the legacy of female empowerment is by promoting women's leadership and representation in various fields. Women should be encouraged to take on leadership roles in politics, business, academia, and other sectors. By having more women in positions of power, we can ensure that their voices are heard, their perspectives are considered, and their contributions are valued.

To achieve this, it is crucial to create a supportive environment that encourages women to pursue leadership positions. This can be done by implementing policies that promote gender equality, providing mentorship and networking opportunities, and challenging gender biases and stereotypes. Additionally, organizations and institutions should actively seek out and promote women's talents and capabilities, ensuring that they have equal opportunities for career advancement.

Advocacy and Activism

ADVOCACY AND ACTIVISM are powerful tools for continuing the legacy of female empowerment. By raising awareness about gender inequality, advocating for women's rights, and challenging discriminatory practices, we can create a more equitable society. This can be done through grassroots movements, social media campaigns, and community engagement.

It is essential to support and amplify the voices of women who are advocating for change. By standing in solidarity with them, we can help bring attention to the issues they are fighting for and contribute to the dismantling of patriarchal structures. This can involve supporting organizations that work towards gender equality, participating in protests and demonstrations, and using our platforms to amplify women's voices.

Mentorship and Support

MENTORSHIP AND SUPPORT play a crucial role in empowering women and helping them navigate the challenges they may face. By providing mentorship opportunities, women can benefit from the guidance and wisdom of those who have walked similar paths before them. Mentors can offer advice, share their experiences, and provide a supportive network for women to lean on.

In addition to mentorship, it is essential to create support systems that address the unique needs and challenges faced by women. This can involve establishing women's networks and organizations, providing resources for childcare and work-life balance, and implementing policies that promote gender equality in the workplace. By creating an environment that supports and uplifts women, we can empower them to reach their full potential.

Celebrating and Honoring Warrior Queens

LASTLY, CONTINUING the legacy of female empowerment involves celebrating and honoring the warrior queens who have paved the way for future generations. By acknowledging their contributions and sharing their stories, we can inspire and empower women to embrace their own strength and resilience. This can be done through literature, art, films, and other forms of media that highlight the achievements of warrior queens.

Furthermore, it is essential to incorporate the history of warrior queens into educational curricula. By teaching young girls and boys about the remarkable women who have shaped African history, we can challenge gender stereotypes and foster a sense of pride and empowerment. By celebrating and honoring warrior queens, we ensure that their legacy lives on and continues to inspire generations to come.

In conclusion, the legacy of female empowerment left by warrior queens in Africa is a powerful testament to the strength and resilience of women throughout history. By continuing their legacy through education, leadership, advocacy, mentorship, and celebration, we can create a more equitable and inclusive society. It is up to each one of us to play our part in empowering women and ensuring that their voices are heard and valued. Together, we can build a future where women have equal opportunities to thrive and make a lasting impact on the world.

Milton Keynes UK
Ingram Content Group UK Ltd.
UKHW010420131223
434231UK00001B/93